Special thanks to former Memphis Mayor, Jim Strickland for his unwavering support of equity, inclusion, diversity, and fairness in the political/social life in Memphis. He was the driving force in the political arena to clear the Memphis landscape of Confederate statues and symbols.

On June 22, 2024, the Pine Hill golf course clubhouse was dedicated to Charles Hudson and Cleophus Hudson, Sr., a father and son team that impacted the game of golf, ultimately making Memphis a better city.

Without the support of Mayor Strickland, Councilwoman Jana Swearengen-Washington, and Edmund Ford, Sr., this historical fete would not have been possible.

*--LaSimba*

On the cover: Two pillars of golf in Memphis' African American golfing community: Robert "Bubba" Jeter and Lonnie "Dollar" Sanders, who introduced, played and taught the game to so many. -- LLMG

Initial Book Design by:
Angelique M. Gray for AngeliQ Creations/Simba Productions

Edited by: Angelique M. Gray and Lee Eric Smith

Final Book Design by: Lee Eric Smith/Fluid Media Group, LLC

Final Editing/Revisions by: Pamela D. Cox

© 2025 by Dr. L. LaSimba Gray, Jr.
ISBN: 9781614226307

All rights reserved. Printed in the United States of America. No part of this book may be used or reproduced, stored, or transmitted in any form or by any means, electronic, mechanical, photocopying, recording, scanning, or otherwise without written permission from the publisher.

# OUT OF BOUNDS

## A History of African Americans and Golf in Memphis, Tennessee

By Rev. Dr. L. LaSimba M. Gray, Jr.

Dedicated to my dear friend,
**Albert "Spooky" Flowers**
**(Dec. 4, 1945 - Nov. 16, 1996),**
who introduced me
to the amazing world of golf.

# Table of Contents

PREFACE ......... 8
FOREWORD ......... 10
ACKNOWLEDGEMENTS ......... 12
INTRODUCTION ......... 16
GOLF COMES TO AMERICA ......... 18
GOLF COMES TO MEMPHIS ......... 20
HOW GOLF ARRIVED IN MEMPHIS ......... 24
ORIGIN OF THE TERM: "CADDIE" ......... 32
THE ACADEMY FOR THE CADDIE ......... 33
THE FLIGHT OF MEMPHIS CADDIES ......... 36
SEGREGATED PARKS AND GOLF COURSES ......... 38
    PROVISION OF GOLF COURSES FOR "NEGROES" ......... 39
SPECIAL TRAVEL ARRANGEMENTS FOR THE AFRICAN AMERICAN GOLFER ......... 49
TEARING DOWN THE WALLS OF SEGREGATION ......... 51
    TIMELINE OF DESEGREGATION OF MEMPHIS GOLF COURSES ......... 55
RACISM CODIFIED BY THE PROFESSIONAL GOLF ASSOCIATION ......... 57
AFRICAN AMERICAN PROFESSIONAL GOLFERS WHO CAME TO MEMPHIS ......... 59
    PHYLLIS G. MEEKINS ......... 60
    PETE BROWN ......... 61
    CHARLIE SIFFORD ......... 62
    LEE ELDER ......... 65
    TIGER WOODS ......... 66
    J.P. THORNTON ......... 78
    BRIA SANDERS ......... 80
DOMINANT PERSONALITIES OF AFRICAN AMERICAN GOLFERS IN MEMPHIS ......... 82
THE MEMPHIS SICKLE CELL ANEMIA OPEN CHARITY GOLF

| | |
|---|---|
| TOURNAMENT | 86 |
| TRIBUTES TO TRUE GOLFING LEGENDS | 96 |
|     CHARLIE WILSON | 100 |
|     BURKINS BROTHERS | 103 |
|     THEODORE "TED" RHODES | 107 |
|     THURMAN "DUNNA" GLASS | 109 |
|     LONNIE "DOLLAR" SANDERS | 112 |
|     ROBERT "BUBBA" JETER | 119 |
|     PLEAS JONES, JR. | 121 |
|     CHARLES HUDSON | 124 |
|     REX CURRY | 126 |
|     JASPER PHILLIPS | 127 |
|     JIMMIE "PECKER" FIELDS | 128 |
|     CELEBRATING THE LIFE OF GENE AUSTIN FENTRESS | 130 |
|     JERRY "CAP" BUTLER | 132 |
| SPECIAL NOTES OF AFRICAN AMERICANS AND GOLF IN MEMPHIS, TENNESSEE | 133 |
| BEST DRESSED GOLFERS IN MEMPHIS | 139 |
| THE MEMPHIS AMATEUR GOLF HALL OF FAME | 141 |
| LEGENDARY AFRICAN AMERICAN GOLFERS OF MEMPHIS AND THE MID-SOUTH | 143 |
| IN MEMORIAM: AFRICAN AMERICAN GOLF LEGENDS OF MEMPHIS | 145 |
| IN MEMORIAM: THE COURAGEOUS MEN WHO FILED THE LAWSUIT WATSON V. CITY OF MEMPHIS | 147 |
| MEMPHIS AREA SANDLOT COURSES | 148 |
| THE PRESERVATION OF HISTORY AT PINE HILL GOLF COURSE | 151 |
| AFTERTHOUGHTS OF THE AUTHOR | 160 |
| ABOUT THE AUTHOR | 163 |
| BIBLIOGRAPHY | 166 |

Dr. L. LaSimba M. Gray, Jr.

# PREFACE
## By James Meredith

The Reverend Dr. L. LaSimba M. Gray, Jr. has completed one of the missing chapters in our struggle for freedom. The desegregation of golf courses on the surface seems insignificant when compared to sit-ins, marches, protests at lunch counters, libraries, schools, and other public accommodations. However, the desegregation of public golf courses played a major role in dismantling white supremacy.

When Dr. Gray approached me about writing the preface, I was forced to revisit my early teens as a caddie at the Kosciusko Country Club in Kosciusko, Mississippi. It was at the Kosciusko Country Club that I was introduced to golf and white supremacy.

It was at that country club that I saw white supremacy in action. I saw the unbridled power of the white power structure, planned on the golf course. I started to caddy at age 14 and became addicted to the game. I played whenever and wherever I could. Caddies were allowed to play on Sunday, but my addiction didn't know the difference between Sunday and Monday. I slipped onto the golf course before it opened and played until I couldn't see after closing.

I personally benefited from golf in several ways: financially, physically, and emotionally. I made money — $.75 per nine holes — and developed a strong work ethic and sense of independence. Walking the course while carrying golf bags, I developed physical stamina. I learned the therapeutic value of self-talk on the golf course. Very often, you knew what to do, but had to talk yourself into doing it.

During my intense days at Ole Miss, a few professors would take me out to play golf on the University Course. Playing golf was my therapy and in some ways enabled me to complete my mission at Ole Miss.

The Rev. Dr. LaSimba Gray guides the reader from the caddy shack to the pinnacles of corporate and political power in the "Capital of Mississippi" — Memphis, Tennessee.

*Out Of Bounds: The History of African Americans and Golf in Memphis*

*Dr. L. LaSimba M. Gray, Jr.*

# FOREWORD
## By Bill Adkins

I learned how to play golf from Rocky Reed, a white golf pro at Riverside Golf Course, when I was 14 years old.

Riverside was a nine-hole course that offered few challenges. It allowed Black players to play the course on a daily basis, something completely uncommon at other courses in Memphis in the era of Jim Crow.

I later graduated to Fuller Golf Course; a course constructed for black golfers. It was a severely tough course, adequately described by the late Sam Qualls as a course purposely designed to discourage black golfers from playing the game. You see, Fuller was hilly, and you could only see the green from the tees on nine holes. Everything else was a dogleg left, which encouraged golfers to learn how to "draw" the ball.

One par-three was situated on a ridge with, maybe, 20 feet of fairway. Missing the green meant you went down the ridge on both sides, as much as 50 yards. I knew the hole was illegal.

But God has a way of taking what's bad and making it for good. Because most black golfers were forced to master Fuller, when they finally were allowed to enter the local Publinx, black golfers from Fuller dominated their white counterparts — much to the chagrin of many of Memphis' finest white golfers.

They were no match for the Fuller golfers.

I was blessed by the Memphis Regional Sickle Cell Council Tournaments held on the Fuller course. I played with Lee Elder and Charlie Sifford, two of the first black golf pros in the PGA.

Lee Elder was the first black golfer to play in the Masters. I actually led Lee Elder by one stroke on the front nine. But he reminded me who he was, finishing 4-under par on the back nine.

Golf has been a major part of my life. The friendships developed were significant on every level of my life and successes. My pastor, our author, Dr. L. LaSimba Gray, was and still is my golf buddy and best friend.

Golf was a welcome relief from the daily struggles we faced in the Civil Rights Movement. We fought together, and we played together. I owe so much to him.

I also owe a lot to golf. Golf teaches discipline. Athleticism is not always helpful in golf. Mental toughness is mandatory.

That mental toughness of golf helped me in the game of life.

I'm so thankful I played the game.

*Dr. L. LaSimba M. Gray, Jr.*

# ACKNOWLEDGEMENTS

I am indebted to the many golfers who met with me at Stein's Restaurant for a "Friday Fish Fry" in May of 2022. Thanks to Charles Hudson and Cornelius Burkins for the follow-up invitations. The attendance was excellent, but the dialogue was better.

In that gathering, there was a solid commitment to preserving the history of African Americans and Golf in Memphis. As painful as that story was, I do not recall one outburst of anger. We celebrated our achievements on and off the golf courses of Memphis.

Individuals brought souvenirs, photos, and scorecards. I have a special thanks to the following individuals:

- Charles Hudson for receiving my many phone calls and making suggestions for this project.
- Andrew "Joe Bear" Bryant, who shared several funeral programs of the deceased golfers of our era.
- The families of Walter Evans, Leon H. Griffin, Gene Fentress, and Albert Flowers.
- Attorney Robert Larry Brown and Dr. Brenda Shaw for photos of my early ventures into managing golf tournaments in Jackson, Tennessee.
- Pleas Jones, Jr. and Cornelius Burkins graciously carved out blocks of time to share their perspectives on this intriguing story of African Americans wanting to compete and enjoy golf in Memphis, Tennessee when the opposition was so entrenched in the Memphis Culture.

Without the phenomenal expertise of my daughter, Angelique M. Gray, in graphics, this project would have been lost on some shelf of my library. I hear her words of encouragement on a daily basis; "Let's get it done, Daddy."

I am indebted to corporate leaders like Tom Shropshire of Miller

Brewing Company, Calvin Vinson of Coors Brewing, and Johnny Arnold of Arnold and Associates. Local supporters included Universal Life Insurance Company, Tri-State Bank, Holiday Inn and Term City Furniture.

The Board of Directors of the Memphis Regional Sickle Cell Council, Inc was a driving force in the success of the Sickle Cell Open Golf Tournament. Ms. Mercury Bowie led the Sickle Cell Booster Club in supportive activities on a year-round basis.

Dr. Joseph Westbrook for his mentoring in program development and implementation. Marjorie Mayhue and Nellie Tate for their commitment to program integrity.

I enjoyed the support of a dedicated staff including Patricia Jackson, Teresa Freeman James, Carolyn Bishop, John Ferguson, and Maurice Estes.

I wish to thank the staff of the Benjamin L. Hooks Library (Memphis Room). William Keys, course manager at Pine Hill, and a tremendous resource on the history of Memphis golf and especially Pine Hill Golf Course. Without his support, I would not have known where to start on this project.

*Photo credits: Robert "Rocky" Jefferson, Pleas Jones Jr., Attorney Robert L. Brown, Faith Griffin Morris, Charles Hudson, Dr. Harry Davis, Rev. Louetta Burkins, Corneilus Burkins, and Ruby Fentress.*

*Dr. L. LaSimba M. Gray, Jr.*

# **ESSENTIAL READING:**

## The 14th Amendment to The Constitution of The United States of America

**Ratified by The Tennessee State Legislature: July 18, 1866 Fully adopted: July 9, 1868**

"*All persons, born or naturalized in the United States and subject to the jurisdiction there of are citizens of the United States, and of the state wherein they reside. No state shall make, or enforce any law, which shall abridge the privileges or immunities of citizens of the United States; nor shall any state deprive any person of life, liberty, or property without due process of law.*"

The 14th Amendment nullified the legal precedent set in the 1857 notorious Dred Scott decision. In this decision, Supreme Court Chief Justice Roger Taney wrote that a black man, even if born free, could not claim the rights of citizenship under the federal constitution.

**In 1868, the 14th Amendment said, "not so."**

# THE HISTORY OF AFRICAN AMERICANS IN GOLF IN MEMPHIS...

# ...HAD NOT BEEN TOLD.

*Dr. L. LaSimba M. Gray, Jr.*

# INTRODUCTION

When the announcement was made in 2021 of the massive renovations of the Pine Hills Golf Course, the thought occurred to me: What will happen to all of that history?

The history of African Americans in golf, which began at Lincoln Park Golf Course (1935), Douglass Golf Course (1951), and the iconic T.O. Fuller Golf Course (1956), had not been told.

I made a phone call to Bobby Hall, a retired sportswriter for *The Commercial Appeal*. My opening question was, "Is there a recorded history of the desegregation of golf in Memphis?" Bobby replied that he was not aware of any such documentation, made a couple of referrals, and wished me well.

The next morning, Bobby called me, exclaiming, "Your question about the desegregation of golf in Memphis is one of the most intriguing I've heard since my retirement." I knew then I had a mission: to document this rich history of African-Americans and golf in Memphis, Tennessee. When I returned to Memphis in 1973, most African Americans who played golf gathered at T. O. Fuller Golf Course. It was the first 18-hole course built for African Americans during segregation. When T. O. Fuller Golf Course closed in 1987, the venue of choice became Pine Hill. Centrally located and easily accessible, Pine Hill was the first municipal golf course in Memphis that allowed African Americans to play. The management
there helped build an atmosphere of fraternal relationships.

Lerone Bennett, the celebrated historian, said, "If African American youth are to make history, they must know their history." The history of African Americans in golf has not been told. As the author of this work, I fear that if it's not documented in 2022, this rich history will be lost to Alzheimer's, amnesia, and the passage of time. What a tragedy it would be if golfers were denied the contributions made by African Americans in Memphis, Tennessee.

# Out Of Bounds: The History of African Americans and Golf in Memphis

From the building of golf courses to the manufacturing of golf clubs, African Americans have been there. We cooked in the country clubs, maintained the courses, carried the bags, cleaned the shoes, found the balls, and read the breaks on the greens. We didn't fight for credit and coverage. We were often told, "Show up, keep up, and shut up."

I am well beyond adhering to those rules and must now tell the story.

From 1896 to 1962, African Americans could not benefit from the Park System and outdoor recreational opportunities provided by taxpayers in Memphis. Golf was first introduced to Memphis via private country clubs in 1896, and the general public was introduced to it via public courses in the early 1900s.

The exclusion from public parks and golf courses was so severe politically that Robert R. Church Sr. built the first park for African Americans on Beale Street with his own money in 1899. Church Park was said to be the only facility of its kind for African Americans in the country, yet it did not include golf.

If the original premise for creating parks and outdoor recreation was for a "healthier Memphis," then the exclusion of African Americans meant their physical and mental health did not matter in Memphis, Tennessee.

For about 66 years, African American golfers were considered "out-of-bounds" in public and private golf clubs in Memphis. The debate continues: "How can the path to the PGA be made smoother? And can we make up for lost time due to racism and blatant discrimination?"

The answers may lie in the newly formed LIV, which provides new options for African American golfers. It began with no exclusion of golfers by race and large financial backing. The LIV and the PGA merged in 2023, pressuring for changes that will benefit those previously declared "out of bounds."

*\*LIV - is the new professional golf tour, financed by the Public Investment Fund, the Sovereign Wealth Fund of Saudi Arabia. Although the LIV and the PGA merged in 2023, the pressure for change will benefit those who have been declared Out of Bounds.*

*Dr. L. LaSimba M. Gray, Jr.*

# GOLF COMES TO AMERICA

On the wings of immigration in the 18th Century, golf made the Transatlantic trip from Europe to America. Scottish immigrants brought the passion for golf and the skills to make needed equipment. Historians suggest that the origins of golf lie in the boredom of shepherds watching sheep and goats. While waiting and watching, these shepherds began to hit rocks with sticks. This pastime soon turned competitive, and the competition spread to various villages in Scotland. It was during these street competitions that the popularity of the game began to grow.

Scotland was an ideal setting for this embryonic stage of golf. The landscape, punctuated with open spaces used for pastures, lacked trees, and the grazing sheep and goats kept the grass trimmed low. This shift from the streets to the pasturelands marked a significant development in the game.

While immigration is recognized for facilitating the transport of golf to America, the role of the cotton trade cannot be overlooked. Merchants, eager to supply the mills of Europe with raw material for fabric, found new supply lines in America, especially in the South. This economic activity inadvertently supported the introduction and growth of golf in the region.

Reportedly, the first golf course outside the United Kingdom was the South Carolina Golf Club in Charleston, South Carolina. From Edinburgh, Scotland, to Charleston, South Carolina, Golf found a new home in America, setting the stage for its expansion and evolution.

*Out Of Bounds: The History of African Americans and Golf in Memphis*

*Dr. L. LaSimba M. Gray, Jr.*

# GOLF COMES TO MEMPHIS

Mr. J. P. Edrington is credited with bringing the game of golf to Memphis.

On December 10, 1896, a select group of Memphians, eager to play golf, organized the Memphis Golf Club, which later became the Memphis Country Club. J. P. Edrington was elected president and soon dominated the club championships, often being compared to golfing legend Bobby Jones.

The first course was laid out at the head of Peabody Avenue (see diagram). Conveniently, J. P. Edrington lived on Peabody, adjacent to the course. W. V. Hoare was elected as the first professional. The original nine holes, located just north of Vance Avenue near East Street, averaged approximately 300 yards in length, and tomato cans served as holes. Golf clubs were scarce, prompting J. P. Edrington to allow members to use his.

By the fall of 1897, the interest in golf had grown significantly in Memphis. Many members purchased their own clubs, cementing golf's place in the city.

The acceptance and growth of golf in Memphis were also influenced by the impact of cotton on the local economy. The surrounding land, once used for cotton cultivation, played a key role. Notably, the Pine Hills Golf Course, now public property, was originally part of a 2000-acre plantation owned by Colonel William Person. Similarly, the Cherokee Country Club originated on farmland near Caperville, east of Memphis; Colonial Country Club was established near Cordova, and Windyke Country Club in the Germantown/Collierville area.

*Out Of Bounds: The History of African Americans and Golf in Memphis*

**J.P. Edrington is credited with introducing golf to Memphis culture in 1896.**

Golf's introduction to America during the post-Reconstruction era of the 19th century coincided with an America deeply entrenched in segregation. The withdrawal of federal troops from the South and the failure of the Freedmen's Bureau to transform Southern society left the region ripe for the resurgence of old social orders.

Historians cite three main reasons for the failure of Reconstruction: convict leasing, sharecropping, and the unchecked terrorism of the Ku Klux Klan. Add to this the segregation in schools, housing, and jobs, along with lynchings, and one finds America struggling to truly free its former slaves.

From 1863 to 1963, freedom for African Americans vacillated between dreams and nightmares. Dreams kept hope alive amidst the harsh reality of second and third-class citizenship. The nightmare manifested daily in employment inequities, lynchings, limited access to capital, and unequal public accommodations.

In Memphis, golf quickly became a segregated haven of Anglo-Saxon society. The Golf Country Clubs emerged as citadels of white supremacy, defining specific roles for African Americans as caddies, cooks, janitors, groundskeepers, and greenskeepers.

In 1900, Memphis began constructing public parks for outdoor recreation. Overton Park allowed non-country club members exposure to golf, yet African Americans were excluded. Riverside was built on the southwest side of Memphis for the growing population, which had reached 102,320 by this time.

In 1899, after numerous failed appeals to city leaders for recreational outlets for African Americans, Robert R. Church Sr. built Church Park on Beale Street. This historic park, built entirely with private funds, did not include a golf course.

Douglas Park, established in 1913 in Northeast Memphis on 53 acres, added a nine-hole golf course in 1951. Lincoln Park, built in 1935 in the Bunkerhills area, originally had a seven-hole course, which was later closed following the construction of the course in Douglas Park.

From 1957 to 1970, the Memphis Park Commission operated the T. O. Fuller Golf Course, an 18-hole course within the city limits, specifically for African Americans. It quickly became a golfing Mecca, attracting players from across the Mid-South for major African American tournaments.

The establishment of T.O. Fuller Golf Course sparked increased interest in golf within the African American community and demands for the right to play at other public golf courses in Memphis. In 1960, Dr. Ike A. Watson Jr., a local dentist and golfer, filed a lawsuit in Federal District Court to end discrimination in the use of public parks and golf courses. The City of Memphis, denying allegations of systematic racism, fought for gradual desegregation, citing "separate but equal" facilities. The U.S. District Court ruled in favor of the City of Memphis, but the plaintiffs appealed. The Sixth Circuit Court of Appeals upheld the District Court's ruling, allowing Memphis to desegregate gradually over a ten-year plan. The plaintiffs then appealed to the United States Supreme Court, which ruled on May 27, 1963, in favor of the plaintiffs: "The City of Memphis had no constitutional grounds to continue excluding African Americans from public golf courses and other recreational outlets based on race."

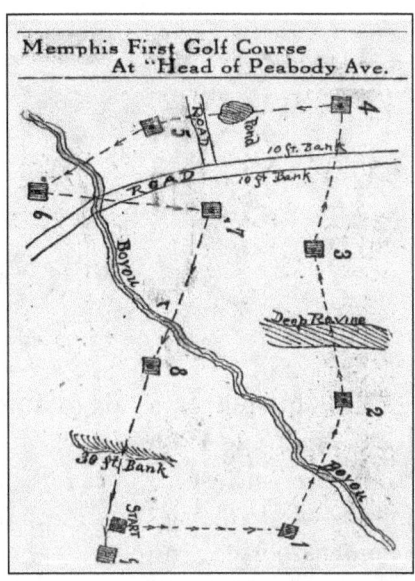
*Memphis' first golf course on Peabody Ave.*

In 1935, the city attempted to build a golf course for African Americans on Ball Road, south of the Army Depot. However, the demands of World War II and the defense industries led to the abandonment of this plan. The golf course for African Americans was eventually built at Lincoln Park, as a seven-hole course.

On January 1, 1962, a historic moment unfolded at Pine Hill, the first public golf course to remove its "Whites Only" sign. Despite the cold 37-degree weather, Cleophus Hudson Sr., Richard Powell, Lawrence Daughtery, and James "Gump" Edwards teed off, marking a significant victory.

*Dr. L. LaSimba M. Gray, Jr.*

# HOW GOLF ARRIVED IN MEMPHIS

Golf hitchhiked a ride to America during the European Migration Era of the 1800s.

The earliest recorded formation of an organized golf club in America was in Charleston, South Carolina in 1786, followed by a club in Savannah Georgia around 1794 or 1795. In Memphis, the first Golf Club was organized in 1896.

Discussing the arrival of golf in America necessitates understanding its connection to the agriculture of the South. European cotton merchants, drawn to the South in pursuit of "White Gold," discovered not only abundant cotton but also vast open spaces of land, ideal for constructing golf courses. The land once used for growing cotton, corn, and soybeans, allowed for the economic development of golf courses.

In the Southwest, the abundance of hickory trees was crucial for producing golf club shafts. Before the advent of steel shafts, these were predominantly made of hickory wood, while the club heads were crafted from persimmon and other hardwoods.

Memphis, renowned as the world's cotton capital, also played a significant role in golf due to its natural resources. E. L. Bruce established the largest hardwood floor manufacturing plant in Memphis in 1921, providing raw materials that also fueled the golf club manufacturing boom of the early 20th century. The Bert Dargie Golf Company, founded in 1908 by Scottish immigrants, became a global leader in golf club manufacturing.

Willie Burkins, Cornelius Burkins, and Dave Alexander, trained by the Dargie Company, became respected African American craftsmen in golf club making and repair. Their expertise was well regarded by PGA members who played in the St. Jude Golf Tournament in Memphis.

John Price "J.P." Edrington, born in Osceola, Arkansas in 1862, was a pivotal figure in Memphis golf. He was educated in Memphis and graduated from J.D. Stewart's University School in 1878. Starting his career in corporate Memphis, he served as Secretary/Treasurer of the Memphis Grocery Company.

Edrington introduced golf to Memphis in 1896 and played a key role in founding the Memphis Country Club. He won the title of "Southern Champion" at the club's links in 1909 and later served as its president. Often compared to the legendary Bobby Jones, founder of the Masters Golf Tournament, Edrington had a profound influence on the Memphis golf scene.

His exposure to golf began in Denver, Colorado, where he encountered the game and acquired a set of clubs made in Scotland. Initially, he loaned his clubs to Memphis residents, sparking their interest until they could purchase their own.

The first golf course in Memphis was constructed at the head of Peabody Avenue (refer to the early course layout). The Commercial Appeal played a significant role in promoting golf in Memphis. On February 1, 1898, the newspaper published an article to introduce Memphis residents to golf, and on May 23, 1897, it printed a full-page ad explaining the game, complete with illustrations and details.

This coverage ignited interest in golf, leading to the organization of three additional golf clubs in Memphis, along with public golf courses. However, during this era, Memphis was a segregated city, with no provisions allowing African Americans to play golf.

## THE DEVELOPMENT OF THE PARK SYSTEM IN MEMPHIS

Following the Civil War and the Reconstruction Era, along with the withdrawal of Federal Troops, Memphis emerged as a haven for newly freed African Americans and European immigrants. This influx led to a building boom that transformed downtown Memphis and its skyline. However, this rapid development created a challenge: overcrowding and a lack of physical space.

Dr. L. LaSimba M. Gray, Jr.

This need for space sparked the urban park movement across the nation. Recognizing the importance of recreational spaces, Memphis initiated its park system in 1895 with a $250,000 bond exclusively earmarked for park development. The city purchased two large tracts of wooded land in East and Southwest Memphis. The eastern tract became Overton Park, named in honor of founding proprietor John Overton.

Overton Park was designed to be the "crown jewel" of the Memphis Park Commission. Its amenities included a golf course, fishing lake, zoological garden, athletic fields, playground, pavilions, and stages for concerts.

In contrast, the larger tract in Southwest Memphis, which would later become Riverside Park, developed more slowly and initially remained a natural park. Riverside Park eventually included a fishing lake, golf course, and pavilions and was posthumously named in honor of civil rights icon Dr. Martin Luther King, Jr.

Despite these developments by the Memphis Park Commission, there was a glaring omission: African Americans were prohibited from attending both public and private parks during the segregation era.

In response to this exclusion, Robert Church Sr., a self-made millionaire, established Church Park in 1899. He purchased a six-acre lot on Beale Street and developed a park, amusement center, and a 2,000-seat auditorium, all without public funding. Church Park, while a symbol of pride, could not fully address the recreational needs of the African American community.

*Out Of Bounds: The History of African Americans and Golf in Memphis*

Due to mounting political pressure, city officials purchased a 53-acre tract of land in Northeast Memphis in 1913 to build Douglas Park. Lincoln Park was later developed in Southwest Memphis, offering tennis, golf, picnic areas, and baseball diamonds.

In 1935, city officials planned a golf course for African Americans on Ball Road adjacent to the Memphis Depot. However, this "Negro Only" golf course never materialized.

It wasn't until 1956 that the State of Tennessee opened the T.O. Fuller Golf Course in the State Park, a unique collaboration between the state and the city to serve the progressive-minded African American community.

The city's attempts to provide equitable access to public parks, golf courses, and recreational facilities were often seen as insufficient. Designated "Negro only" days at the zoo, art gallery, and Mid-South Fair, combined with Douglas, Lincoln, and T.O. Fuller Parks, were viewed as token gestures to a population that constituted 49 percent of Memphis in 1900.

It was only after Dr. Ike A. Watson Jr., a local dentist and golfer, filed a federal lawsuit in 1960 that significant change occurred. The lawsuit made its way through the U.S. Court of Appeals for the 6th Circuit in 1962.

The City of Memphis sought to delay desegregation in the use of public parks and recreational facilities, but in 1963, the United States Supreme Court ruled that all racial barriers in the use of public parks and publicly operated recreational outlets must be abolished.

*Dr. L. LaSimba M. Gray, Jr.*

# THE TIMELINE FOR GOLF IN MEMPHIS

**1922** — Chickasaw Country Club Founded.

**1913** — Ridgeway Country Club Founded.

**1913** — Memphis Country Club and Colonial Country Club Founded.

**1912** — First Municipal Golf Course (Overton) is built for the public.

**1899** — Robert R. Church, Sr. built Church Park and Auditorium* on Beale Street for negroes after Memphis Park Commission refused to build parks for negroes.

**1896** — December 10, 1896 ---- J. P. Edrington Introduces Golf In Memphis, Tennessee.

\* Robert Church, Sr. used his own money to fund the project. The Church Park and Auditorium in Memphis was the only business venture of its kind in America.

*Out Of Bounds: The History of African Americans and Golf in Memphis*

1932 — Pine Hill Golf Course Founded.

1935 — Lincoln Park Golf Course Opened For Negroes (7 Holes)

1941 — Pine Hill Golf Course Becomes A Property of The Memphis Park Commission.

1951 — Douglas Park Golf Course Opened For Negroes (9 Holes)

1957 — T. O. Fuller Golf Course opened for Negroes (18 Holes).

1958 — The Binghampton Civic League Petitioned the Memphis Park Commission For Full Integration of All Tax-Supported Facilities In Memphis.

1962 — Pine Hill Golf Course Was Desegregated Along With Riverside Golf Course

1963 — All Public Golf Courses In Memphis ordered desegregated by the Supreme Court of the United States.

*Dr. L. LaSimba M. Gray, Jr.*

# THE EMERGENCE OF THE CADDIE AND THE ACADEMY FOR CADDIES

*Out Of Bounds: The History of African Americans and Golf in Memphis*

*Dr. L. LaSimba M. Gray, Jr.*

# ORIGIN OF THE TERM: "CADDIE"

In the Scottish Language, the term Caddie was derived in the 17th century from a French word: Cadet. It originally meant a student officer. It evolved to mean someone who performed odd jobs.

By the beginning of the 19th century, the term "caddie" was commonly used to refer to someone who carried clubs for a golfer. But what exactly is the role of a caddie?

A caddie's responsibilities include:
- Carrying the golfer's bag of clubs,
- Keeping the golf balls in focus during play,
- Ensuring the golf ball is clean on the green,
- Keeping the clubs clean, and
- Walking ahead of the player to calculate yardage to the pin and identify potential hazards.

The extent of a caddie's role can vary depending on the relationship between the caddie and the golfer. In some instances, a caddie may be consulted for their opinion on the distance to the pin or to help read the level and break of the putt on the green.

Historically, the most common rule adhered to by the PGA and golf clubs regarding caddies was the rule of "ups": show up, shut up and keep up.

*"It was through caddying that I was not only introduced to golf, but to life."*
*Attorney Herman Morris*
*Morris Law Firm Memphis, TN*

# THE ACADEMY FOR THE CADDIE

The Caddie played a major role in the development of golf. The caddie, typically a young African American boy aged 10 to 14, was a golfer's attendant.

The entry-level position was known as a "bag toter" or "ball shagger," and it took time to develop into a bona fide caddie. By the beginning of the 19th century, the term caddie was applied to someone who carried clubs for a golfer.

A caddie had to learn the game of golf, the expected behavior to navigate the landscape of the country club, the layout of the golf course, and the breaks on the greens. Distinguishing a caddie from a mere "bag toter" were skills like club selection and determining the distance to the green. All country clubs had an area near the clubhouse designated as the Caddie Shack, or a waiting area for caddies.

The concept of an Academy for Caddies was realized through the informal training of young caddies by older, experienced ones. Without formal lesson plans or final exams, young caddies gradually developed their skills. As they progressed from bag toters, their financial benefits increased, and their social standing was elevated.

Several jobs at the country club were aspirations for a caddie: caddie master, head chef, head janitor, club steward, greenskeeper, and superintendent of grounds. The country club was not just a place of employment; the Caddie Shack was a gateway to building relationships extending beyond the golf course.

The work was hard, long, and clean, typically spanning from sun-up to sundown, but it was preferable to chopping or picking cotton.

Herman Morris, a prominent lawyer and former CEO of Memphis Light Gas and Water, reflected on his caddying experiences at Chickasaw

Country Club, saying, "We were introduced to golf, but more importantly, to life. We made money and gained invaluable knowledge about life."

The Reverend Willie Ward, a retired executive with Federal Express and Pastor of Mt. Pisgah C.M.E. Church, echoed these sentiments. He recounted the economic impact of caddying and how it enabled him to shop in thrift stores and present himself as one of the best-dressed young men in the neighborhood.

"I received advice from various individuals at Chickasaw that benefited me professionally and personally," he said.

"We would get paid and walk over to Summer Avenue and shop in the thrift stores," Ward said. "We would go straight to the cleaners to drop off our second-hand clothing. When we picked them up, they looked like new clothing. We were known in the neighborhood to be the best-dressed young men."

Caddies were in a position to financially assist their families with food, bills, and other expenses, and importantly, support themselves with school supplies and lunch money.

Veteran caddies often advised, "Don't spend all your money in one place, give some to your momma, and save some for a rainy day."

To appreciate the impact of a caddie's compensation, it must be viewed in context.

In Binghampton, the Scott Street Market offered a limited number of jobs, like cleaning the grounds and unloading produce trucks. A young man could make a penny per watermelon he tossed from the trucks to waiting stackers. With a good breakfast and a strong determination, a 10- or 12-year-old could toss 100 melons per day and collect one dollar for his efforts.

The other options were to chop or pick cotton in rural Shelby County and Eastern Arkansas. The rate of pay was .25 to .40 per hour for 10 hours a day for chopping cotton; picking cotton paid by the pound, depending on what plantation you picked cotton.

The range was .30 to .40 per pound. Most adults could pick 200 pounds, but youth struggled to pick 100 pounds.

The minimum wage in 1940 was .30 per hour. In 1950, the minimum wage was .75 per hour. In 1960, the minimum wage was raised to $1.00 per hour.

The overwhelming number of jobs for African Americans paid minimum wage. Jobs that paid above minimum wage were called "good jobs" and those that paid below minimum were called "nickel jobs."

Caddies in Memphis might not have become millionaires, but they found an alternative to cotton fields and the limited wages of unsanitary and dangerous work. It was prestigious to say, "I work at Memphis Country Club" or "I am the head chef at Chickasaw Country Club."

The purchasing power of the dollar in the 1950s and 1960s, when compared to today's economy, highlights the financial significance of a caddie's earnings. For example, one dollar in 1950 could buy two movie tickets, a pound of coffee, or four gallons of gas.

In 1983, the Augusta National Country Club dropped its requirement that Masters participants had to use club caddies. This was the beginning of the end for the legendary caddies of the Masters. Touring pros soon started to bring their personal caddies. Soon thereafter, the African American caddies in white jumpsuits were replaced by European Americans in white jumpsuits.

Legends like Hard Rock were marginalized and forced into retirement. They spent their later years on social security and periodic gifts from men they had helped to make millions. He had looped for Ben Hogan and Sam Snead.

In Memphis, the decline of the caddie was directly connected to the advent of the golf cart and range-finding technology. Caddie shacks were replaced with sheds for golf carts. Needless to say, when the face of caddying changed, so did the compensation. White caddies can now become millionaires.

*Dr. L. LaSimba M. Gray, Jr.*

# THE FLIGHT OF MEMPHIS CADDIES

| CADDIE | GOLF COURSE | PROFESSION |
|---|---|---|
| Herman Morris | Chickasaw | Lawyer, CEO of MLG&W and City Attorney for Memphis, Tennessee |
| Rev. Willie Ward | Chickasaw | Corporate Leader at FedEx and Pastor in the CME Church |
| Charlie Wilson | Chickasaw | Golfing Legend/ Logistics for Kimberly Clark |
| Andrew Bryant | Cherokee & Fox Meadows | Logistics/Shipping |
| Albert Flowers | Cherokee/ Windyke | Educator/Business Owner |
| Willie Flowers | Cherokee/ Windyke | Memphis Firefighter/Accountant |
| Cornelius Burkins | Colonial | Skilled Craftsman (golf club maker) |
| Willie Burkins | Colonial | Skilled Craftsman (golf club maker) |
| Coach John Crawford | Colonial | High School Coach and Art Teacher |
| Pleas Jones, Jr. | Douglas/T. O. Fuller | Business Owner/Hall of Fame golfer |
| Charlie Holmes | Cherokee | Independent grocer |
| Rickey Hudson | Douglas/T.O. Fuller | Medical Doctor |

## Out Of Bounds: The History of African Americans and Golf in Memphis

| CADDIE | GOLF COURSE | PROFESSION |
|---|---|---|
| Fred Jones, Jr. | Memphis Country Club | Founder, Southern Heritage Classic |
| Polk McCray | Ridgeway | Civil Service, Hall of Fame golfer |
| Jake Flowers | Chickasaw | Civil Service |
| Lonnie "Dollar" Sanders | Memphis Country Club | Business Owner/ Hall of Fame golfer |
| Dave Alexander | Colonial | Master Craftsman (golf club maker) |
| Lonnie Latham | Chickasaw | Leader in Higher Education: Executive Leader at the University of Memphis |
| Rev. E. F. Gray | Cherokee/ Windyke | Mortician/ Pastor |
| Eddie Lowe | Douglas | Corporate Leader, FedEx |
| Odell Price | Colonial | Mass Transportation City of Memphis |
| Lee Price | Colonial | U.S. Postal Services President of Postal Workers Union |
| Wendell Payton | Colonial | Majored in Business at Lane College and became a pioneering account executive at WMC-TV |
| James Meredith | Kosciusko Country Club | Activist and First Black student at Ole Miss (1962) |
| Tony James | Memphis Country Club | Financial Advisor and Banking Consultant |
| Ossie "Moonman" Bell | T. O. Fuller | United States Postal Worker and Shelby County Sheriff's Office |

*Dr. L. LaSimba M. Gray, Jr.*

# SEGREGATED PARKS AND GOLF COURSES

# PROVISION OF GOLF COURSES FOR "NEGROES" (1900 - 1963)

At the end of World War II, there was a new resolve for civil rights in Memphis. African Americans had fought Hitler and Nazism in Europe, the assault on Pearl Harbor in the Pacific Theater of war, and many resolved that racism, and discrimination made a formidable enemy. Joe Louis, the legendary Heavyweight Boxing Champion, saw racism in golf as the "Next Hitler to be defeated."

In Memphis, the demands for better golf courses intensified and manifested itself in political pressure. The earliest known effort to provide a golf course for African Americans took place in 1935 – when the city purchased a tract of land on Ball Road on the South Side of the Memphis Depot. This project has been referred to as the "Golf Course that never was." It was never developed, and the city turned to Lincoln Park, which opened in 1935.

Lincoln Park, built exclusively for African Americans on Blakemore and Menager Streets in the Bunker Hill Area, included a 7-hole golf course that was vehemently rejected by the African American community as unfair and grossly inadequate.

The Memphis Park Commission then built a much better golf course for African Americans at Douglas Park in North Memphis. This course had nine holes and was much better designed to meet the golfing needs of African Americans. The Douglas Park Golf Course opened in 1951, and consequently, the golf course at Lincoln Park was closed.

The political pressure increased as the interest in golf continued to grow among African Americans. The City of Memphis developed an unprecedented relationship with T.O. Fuller State Park, building a golf course for African Americans in a Tennessee State Park in 1955-1956.

## THE MECCA OF T.O. FULLER GOLF COURSE

The T.O. Fuller Golf Course was built in a 1,138-acre park named in honor of Dr. Thomas Oscar Fuller (1857-1942), a minister, author, President of Howe Institute, and pastor of First Baptist Church Lauderdale.

The layout of the golf course made it one of the most unique courses on the Negro golfing Chitlin Circuit. In 1956, the City of Memphis funded the construction of a golf course exclusively for "Negroes" in T.O. Fuller State Park. The Memphis Park Commission operated the course from 1957 to 1974, when the city relinquished the management to the State of Tennessee.

The golf course became the "golfing mecca" of the Mid-South for African Americans. It was the first state park east of the Mississippi River for African Americans. In addition to the golf course, the park's amenities included picnic areas, a large pavilion, a softball field, basketball courts, a swimming pool, and a trail for the blind.

Hole No. 1 was a par three with out-of-bounds on the right. The course was considered the most challenging in the Mid-South. In a 1978 survey by the Commercial Appeal to determine the most challenging holes of golf in Memphis, T.O. Fuller was home to two of the most challenging holes.

The most challenging was No. 12: a 430-yard dogleg left hole. It had a narrow fairway with out-of-bounds on both sides and then an elevated green with a sand trap to the right.

The second most challenging at Fuller was the 13th hole, infamously called "the Eagle's Nest." It was a par 3, with very little fairway and a notable sand trap on the left between the cart path and the elevated green.

This hole often had pre-set limits on strokes in tournaments to keep play moving.

*Out Of Bounds: The History of African Americans and Golf in Memphis*

Lee Elder, playing at T.O. Fuller in 1975, commented, "I've played all over the nation and never played the No. 1 hole as a par 3."

Ike A. Hentrel, upon his return to Memphis and playing T.O. Fuller for the first time, lamented, "This course was designed to make Black folk quit golf." During the survey, Pleas Jones Jr. declared holes 12 and 13 as two of the toughest in the nation. "Let anybody birdie either one of those and you will hear about it for a while." In 2011, the State of Tennessee closed the golf course during a budget crunch after a string of deficit operating years. Johnny Scott, the managing pro, initiated a petition drive to save the historic course to no avail.

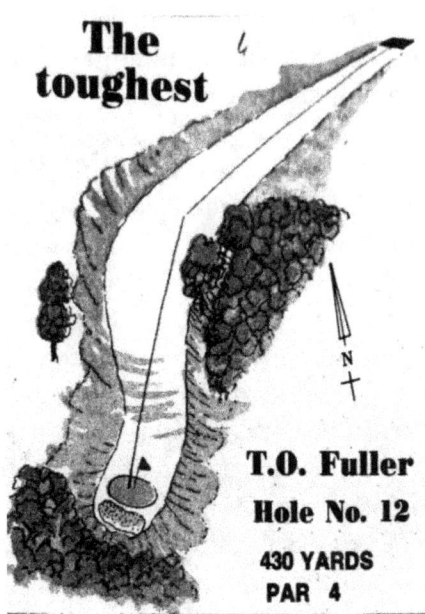

The toughest

T.O. Fuller
Hole No. 12
430 YARDS
PAR 4

The iconic Memphis stop on the African American tour was laid to rest, and now beneath the wildflowers, weeds, and wetland, there lies 55 years of African American golfing history that welcomed all races of people to come inside the ropes.

When T.O. Fuller closed, Pine Hill became the favorite course for African Americans. Centrally located and easily accessible from the I-240 interstate, Pine Hill drew older legends like Saulsberry Johnson, Bubba Jeter, Dollar Saunders, Dalton Nickleberry, Odessa Dickens, Annie Green, Cleophus Hudson, Charles Holmes, Jimmie "the Pecker" Fields, and Calvin Porter.

Memphis was ideally located to develop a strong African American professional class. This group had a new resolve to gain equity based on votes and taxes.

Memphis became the hub for African American culture, political, and economic development. The epicenter was Beale Street.

At the turn of the 20th century, 40 physicians, seven dentists, and 12 lawyers made Memphis their home. Many of the activists who challenged the Laws of Jim Crow in Memphis emerged from this group of professionals.

The group of military veterans who returned from World War II and the Korean conflict gave leadership to dismantle segregation in Memphis. Attorneys Ben L. Hooks, A. W. Willis, Jesse H. Turner, H.T. Lockhart, Russell B. Sugarmon, Rev. Roy Love, and Rev. Henry C. Bunton made the biggest push for political power in 1959 by running the famous "Volunteer Ticket."

It was all Memphians, Black Democrats and Republicans joining together to get African Americans elected to public offices. In July of 1959, a big rally was held at Mason Temple featuring Mahalia Jackson, a 1,000-member choir, and the young Dr. Martin Luther King, Jr.

This rally had a twofold purpose: to raise money and energize the African American voters of Memphis. Promoted as the "Freedom Rally," it did not succeed in electing African Americans to office, but it did increase the voting roles in Memphis to 55,000 African Americans. These new voters became levels of power in the design to make Memphis a truly integrated society.

From public schools, the struggle shifted to parks, golf courses, and public facilities of recreation and entertainment. In 1960, Dr. I.A. Watson, Jr., a dentist and golfer, filed a lawsuit in the United States District Court for the Western District of Tennessee seeking the desegregation of all municipal parks, golf courses, and other city-owned and operated recreational facilities. The case made its way to the United States Supreme Court in 1963. It was argued on April 17-18, 1963, and ruled on May 27, 1963.

The ruling stated: since the City of Memphis had completely failed to demonstrate any compelling or convincing reason for further delay in the desegregation of parks, golf courses, and other publicly owned recreation outlets, the continued denial to petitioners of the use of the city facilities solely because of race was without warrant.

**Special Note:** The legendary, iconic, historical T.O. Fuller Golf Course was closed in 2011 without a fight. There were no pickets, marches, demonstrations, nor lawsuits.

The reason for the lack of protests may well have been because African American golfers now have several options. African Americans could play at any public golf course in Memphis and at a few country clubs. The walls of segregation had been torn down.

In 2011, when the T.O. Fuller Golf Course ran up a $586,434 deficit, more than twice its $287,951 income, the plan was set in motion to end golf and convert the course into a natural area. The days of the par 72, 5,986-yard golf course had come to an end.

Birds of various species can be observed dwelling in what was once named the best golf course in the Tennessee Parks System (1998). Quails, cranes, hawks (red-tailed), and buzzards can be seen all over the newly converted wetlands.

Tom Chartier commented as he watched a giant egret fly away, "These days that's about the closest thing to a birdie to be found at the old golf course."

## HARDSCRABBLE AND SANDLOT GOLF COURSES

African American golfers had very limited opportunities to play golf in Memphis. There was the practice of Country Clubs allowing African American caddies to play on Mondays when most clubs were closed. This opportunity sparked a greater interest in golf, leading to the development of the "Sandlot" golf course. The open spaces of school playgrounds and Memphis City Parks made for ideal sandlot golfing.

A sandlot, in its classical sense, is a vacant lot used for unorganized sports. Youth would gather in these lots to play baseball, softball, football, and eventually, golf emerged as a sport of interest.

The construction of a sandlot golf course required an open field, a lawn mower, a tin can, a cane, or a straight stick with a rag. In some instances, developers dug a hole and placed the stick in the ground.

In many African American communities, one could see these waving flags punctuating the landscape on vacant lots.

The west side of the Memphis Depot between Ball Road and Dunn Avenue provided space for sandlot football, softball, and golf. The developers of this site were James Field, Arthur Gross, Robert Helmes, E.F. Gray, and Charles Holmes.

One of the attractive aspects of Sandlot Golf was its uniqueness. Local residents would gather to watch out of pure curiosity. Many observers would walk away, lamenting, "I don't see the sense in hitting a little white ball as far as you can walk to find it, hit it again and knock it into a hole." Those bitten by the golfing bug kept playing sandlot golf until Pine Hill and other public golf courses opened to African Americans.

In 1898, the very first sandlot golf course was allowed to develop at the Memphis Driving Park on North Parkway East. Frank G. Jones offered the space and later extended the use of his Club House to these pioneering golfers. The Memphis Country Club was established by these efforts on Southern Ave in the Buntyn Community.

Sandlot Golf Courses were established in African American neighborhoods, mostly where caddies lived and wanted to play golf. Golf courses, both public and private, existed throughout the city of Memphis, but African Americans could not play on these courses until 1962. Therefore, these "makeshift" courses provided excellent venues for practice and play:

### The Holiday/Elliston Heights Sandlot Course

This course was established on the east side of Perry Road between Ball and Dunn Roads. Its elongated shape made it ideal, stretching over two city blocks. The United States Government maintained the property adjacent to the Army Depot (the Memphis Depot property).

E.F. Gray and Charles Holmes led the mission of building a golf course for the neighborhood. The course was built with the help of Arthur Gross, Vernon Gross, James Fields, and Robert Helms from Holiday Heights. The Johnson Brothers: Tommy, Clyde, and Charles covered the area north of Elliston Road. Weekly maintenance involved cutting the greens and saving the flags. The elongated course was cut by the US government.

### The Castalia Sandlot Course

Behind the Castalia Supermarket in a vacant field lay the Castalia Sandlot Course. This course was built and maintained by Andrew "Joe Bear" Bryant, Roy Scott, Robert Dolman, and Percy Dolman.

### The White Station Sandlot Golf Course

The site where the Home Depot Hardware store now stands was once the location of the African American youth of White Station's sandlot golf course. Consisting of only two holes, it provided endless enjoyment and was built by Willie Burkins, Cornelius Burkins, and Dave Alexander. Reflecting on this, Cornelius said, "We had to use sling blades to get the grass down."

## The Douglas Sandlot Golf Course

This course existed in the Douglas community prior to the city golf course being built there in 1951. Designed by Dollar Sanders, it aimed to teach golf to neighborhood youth and adults, cut out of the Athletic Fields of Douglas High School. Three of the most accomplished golfers to play there were Pleas Jones Jr., Dalton Nickleberry, Sr., and Odessa Dickens.

## The Lincoln Park Sandlot Golf Course

Lincoln Park's Sandlot Golf Course existed before the city of Memphis built a seven-hole golf course there in 1935. The city, under great protest, closed Lincoln Park Golf Course in 1951. Remnants of the seven holes remained and were used by neighborhood golfers for practice and a few bets.

Following the Supreme Court ruling of 1963, Memphis public golf courses opened to African Americans, and the sandlot golf courses became overgrown with grass and weeds, ultimately being abandoned.

*Dr. L. LaSimba M. Gray, Jr.*

# OUT OF BOUNDS IN PARKS GOLF COURSES IN MEMPHIS

In 1900, African Americans made up 49% of the Memphis population. The demand for outdoor recreation was at the center of urban planning for a healthy city. Public and private entertainment parks were being built to meet the physical and psychological needs of the citizens.

There was a great yearning for "open green space." The Memphis Park Commission responded to the needs by providing outlets in golf, baseball, hiking, cycling, and picnicking. There were private parks that offered concerts, exhibitions, and some of the finest harness racing in the country. Horse racing was second to none and rivaled only by the Kentucky Derby.

African Americans observed these phenomenal developments but were reminded they could not attend. They were not included in the urban plan to enhance the physical and psychological development of Memphians, despite paying taxes, working the labor-intensive jobs required to operate the City of Memphis, and observing the law.

In 1899, Robert R. Church, the first African American millionaire in the South, invested $100,000 in a 6-acre private park and Civic Center on Beale Street. This park was established to meet the physical and psychological needs of African Americans without an apology.

However, Church Park did not solve the racial inequities created by the Memphis Park Commission. A compromise was reached on the premise that if African Americans could not have access to the golf courses, parks, and recreation outlets designed for "whites only," at least comparable outlets should be provided for their exclusive use.

In 1913, the city established a park in the northeast section of Memphis and named it Douglas Park. While this facility provided some recreational outlets, it did not include golf.

It would be thirty-eight years before a nine-hole golf course was added in 1951. The Douglas Golf Course was a temporary fix, but the political pressure continued. The City of Memphis entered into a unique collaboration between the State of Tennessee and the City of Memphis.

In 1956, Memphis funded the construction of an 18-hole golf course in T.O. Fuller State Park, exclusively for African Americans. One of the loyal patrons of T.O. Fuller Golf Course was Dr. Ike A. Watson Jr., a local dentist.

Watson traveled the Negro Chitlin circuit to play on a variety of golf courses but could only play at T.O. Fuller in Memphis. In 1960, Dr. Watson filed a lawsuit in the Federal District Court in Memphis. This lawsuit placed Memphis in the midst of a growing number of cities challenged for discriminatory practices in outdoor recreation.

Between 1947 and 1963, 23 lawsuits were filed in Federal Courts to integrate public golf courses in America. It was during this same era that the Montgomery Bus Boycott took place and Lemoyne College and Owen College students protested discrimination in the public library system and lunch counters in downtown Memphis.

The local NAACP Memphis Branch, led by military veterans including Ben L. Hooks, Jesse Turner, Sr., Archie W. Willis, H.T. Lockhart, and Russell B. Sugarmon, solicited the Legal Defense Fund of New York to get involved.

Initially, Thurgood Marshall thought the resources and time could be better spent on broader issues affecting African Americans. However, the greater wisdom of the Legal Defense Fund prevailed, and Marshall signed on.

The agreed-upon strategy focused on the constitutional rights of African Americans guaranteed by the 14th Amendment, which confirmed the citizenship of the ex-enslaved: "All persons born or nationalized in the United States, and subject to the jurisdiction thereof, are citizens of the United States."

Dr. Ike A. Watson lost his case in the district court in Memphis. Federal Judge Boyd supported the Memphis Park Commission's gradual plan of desegregation. The plaintiffs appealed to the Sixth Circuit Court of Appeals, which upheld the lower court's ruling, meaning segregation would continue until 1971, another ten years. The plaintiff appealed to the Supreme Court.

The Supreme Court of the United States heard the case and ruled in favor of the plaintiffs, ordering Memphis to desegregate golf courses and all recreational outlets. This victory made Dr. Ike A. Watson, Jr., a hero in the Memphis Golfing Community and an icon in the Civil Rights Community.

Following the Montgomery Bus Boycott victory in 1955, and the historic March on Washington on August 28, 1963, Dr. Martin Luther King Jr. emerged as a national leader for civil rights. He joined the ranks with Roy Wilkins, Whitney Young, Roy Innis, and A. Philip Randolph.

Dr. King added his voice to the national call for a Civil Rights Bill. President Lyndon B. Johnson, recognizing the need, passed the 1964 Civil Rights Bill. Later, Dr. King visited President Johnson and requested a Voting Rights Bill.

Realizing he had spent much political capital, President Johnson said, "I just passed the Civil Rights Bill and now I don't have the votes." When Dr. King insisted, President Johnson urged, "Martin, go back to the South and make me pass the Voting Rights Bill." Dr. King left the White House, mentally planning the March from Selma to Montgomery, which took place from March 7 to March 21, 1965.

That March gave President Johnson the public outrage he needed. When Alabama State Troopers brutally suppressed the marchers on "Bloody Sunday," it was seen by millions on national television and aroused public opinion. President Johnson went on national television on March 15, 1965, and announced his support for a new Voting Rights Bill, stating, "There is no Negro problem. There is no Southern problem. There is only an American problem." He continued, "Their cause must be our cause. We must overcome the crippling legacy of bigotry and injustice. We shall overcome!"

The Voting Rights Act passed in August 1965, changing the political landscape of the South. African Americans were elected to the highest offices in cities and states. Thanks to the 1965 Voting Rights Act, African Americans are now able to elect public servants who empower them not only to play at golf courses but also to manage them.

Jesse L. Jackson said it best when he declared, "Hands that once picked cotton now can pick Presidents, Mayors, and Judges."

# SPECIAL TRAVEL ARRANGEMENTS FOR THE AFRICAN AMERICAN GOLFER

The African American Golfer always lived under the cloud of segregation. This required skills to navigate the rules of the Jim Crow Era.

There were always boundaries imposed by racial limitations, and exclusions were simply a part of life. On a daily basis, the African American golfer had to make conscious efforts to stay within bounds.

Golf tournaments were major attractions for competition and companionship. The Memphis African American golfers used word of mouth to find safe places to eat and lodge as they traveled to various African American golf tournaments in cities like St. Louis, Chicago, Atlanta, Little Rock, New Orleans, Memphis, Birmingham, and Nashville.

Travel by automobile required careful planning for gas stations, restaurants, motels, and hotels. The rules of Jim Crow were strictly enforced, and often these golfers had to pack their lunches and were denied routine services available to other tourists.

In 1936, Victor Green, an African American U.S. Postal employee in Harlem, N.Y., published the first guide for Metropolitan N.Y. He later expanded the coverage areas to include every state. This guide was necessary during the Jim Crow era due to discrimination, intimidation, and blatant racial violence.

*Dr. L. LaSimba M. Gray, Jr.*

The Green Book was vital to interstate travel for the African American motorist from 1936 to 1964. The guide warned of towns that must be avoided at sundown and provided lodging reservations, driving tips, tourist-homes, barber shops, beauty parlors, friendly service stations, and taverns. It also served as a tour guide for places of interest to African Americans.

As a marketing strategy, ESSO Standard Oil Company sponsored the Green Book and distributed it to African Americans, soliciting the patronage of African American travelers.

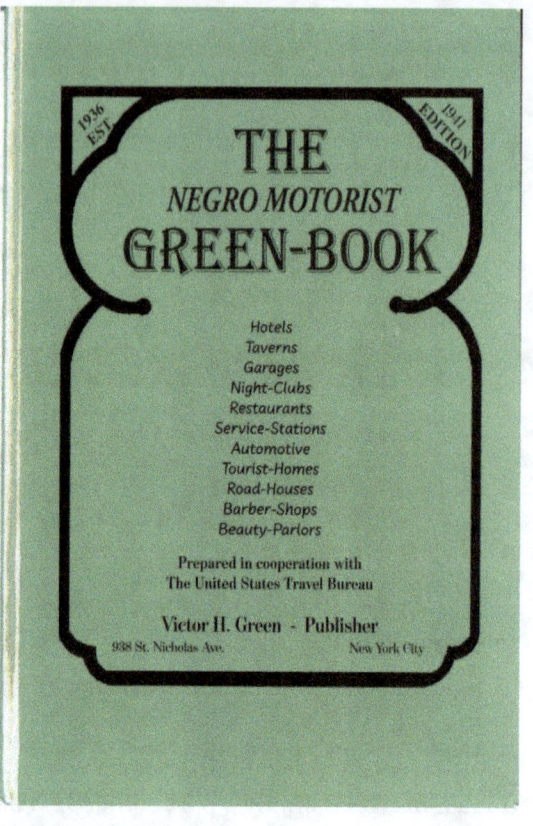

Victor Green wrote, prior to his death in 1960, "When we as a race will have equal opportunities and privileges, The Green Book will no longer be necessary." Following the creation of the Interstate Highway system in 1956 and the passing of the 1964 Civil Rights Bill, The Green Book ceased publication after 1964.

In Memphis, TN, Dr. H.H. Johnson's residence was used regularly because the Heavyweight Boxing Champion Joe Louis could not stay at the Peabody Hotel.

*Tourist homes were private homes that would rent rooms to African American Travelers.

# TEARING DOWN THE WALLS OF SEGREGATION ON PUBLIC GOLF COURSES IN MEMPHIS

Edmond Orgel won the 1955 Memphis Mayoral race with a large African American vote.

Attorney H.T. Lockhart, president of the Memphis Branch of the NAACP, immediately wrote two letters to the 'Powers-that-Be' in Memphis. He addressed the Memphis Park Commission and the Memphis School Board, urgently requesting a meeting to discuss full integration.

As the basis for the requested meeting, Lockhart cited the United States Supreme Court ruling handed down on November 7, 1955, which declared segregation unconstitutional in publicly owned parks, golf courses, playgrounds, and swimming pools. This ruling, an extension of the landmark Brown v. Board of Education decision of 1954, came down two days before the Mayoral election, making Lockhart's timing perfect.

On November 30, 1955, the front-page story of the Commercial Appeal was titled "INTEGRATION SOUGHT," serving as a rallying cry for white Memphis to wake up.

Most white citizens were infuriated and angered by the mere suggestion of integration. The old mentality of Dixie could not fathom African Americans on the same golf course with whites unless they were caddies or greenskeepers.

This notion of race mixing had a better chance up North but not in the "Bluff City." Members of the White Citizens Council and other pro-segregation groups attended city council meetings and Memphis Park Commission meetings to voice their opposition to integration.

Meanwhile, across town, a group of 31 African American Civic Clubs drafted petitions calling for improvements at parks designated for "Negroes."

These parks were often mere vacant lots without restroom facilities or drinking water. A local media survey revealed emphatically that these parks were separate but in no way equal.

A week after Attorney Lockhart's letter reached the Memphis Park Commission, 400 white citizens attended the regularly scheduled meeting, fiercely protesting the integration of all park facilities. Harry W. Pyle, Chairman of the "Pro-Southerners," questioned the NAACP's representation of African Americans in Memphis, stating that his organization had a membership exceeding 10,000 members.

The attending commissioners voted unanimously to table the letter from the NAACP, meaning no action would be taken on full integration in Memphis. When the fuss and fury ended, some thought integration was a dead issue. However, the Supreme Court Ruling was alive and well.

In addition to the United States Supreme Court Ruling, the late Mayor Frank Tobey had invited the Central State Golf Association to hold its annual golf tournament in Memphis. The challenges were twofold: The Central State Golf Tour was an all-African American Golfing Tournament, and it required an 18-hole course.

Douglas Golf Course, with only nine holes, was inadequate to host a national tournament. When Mayor Orgel learned of this invitation, he felt the City of Memphis was obligated to honor it. Unable to rent a Country Club, he was left with one option: schedule the tournament at one of the city-owned 18-hole courses. Once the invitation was made public, white opposition resolved to prevent the tournament from being played on a public golf course in Memphis.

Robert Wright, President of the Sam Qualls Golf Club scheduled to host the tournament, went into damage control. He pledged to conduct a fine tournament that would reflect positively on Memphis and cited successful tournaments held in cities like Denver, Atlanta, Jacksonville, Dallas, St. Louis, and Minneapolis.

During this period of uncertainty, *The Commercial Appeal* and *The Memphis Press-Scimitar* wrote editorials appealing for civility and support of the five-day tournament, scheduled for July 16-20, 1956. The editorials clarified that hosting the Central State Golf Tournament on a white-only golf course did not mean integration of Memphis Public golf courses.

The Central State Golf Tournament was conducted at the Audubon Golf Course without a glitch or any incidents of violence, as Robert Wright had pledged. The tournament was covered by local media, with *The Commercial Appeal* reporting the winners: Elton Grandberry as Champion, followed by Robert "Bubba" Jeter in second place, and Gail Patton from St. Louis winning the women's division.

The letter from Attorney Lockhart was still on file at the Memphis Park Commission, and the desire to play on the public golf courses in Memphis was intensifying, while patience was growing thin in the African American Community.

In May of 1960, the Memphis Branch of the NAACP filed a lawsuit in Federal Court on behalf of eleven plaintiffs, including Dr. Ike A. Watson, Jr., Dr. T.W. Northcross, Dr. Arthur E. Horne, Dr. W.O. Speight, Melvin Malunda, Johnny Gholston, Harold Gholston, Alfred Haynes, Jr., John Rogers, Thomas Pugh, and Curtis King. The suit sought to desegregate the Memphis parks, golf courses, swimming pools, and all public facilities in the Memphis Recreational Department.

The lawsuit was heard in Federal Court on June 15, 1961. The City of Memphis argued against immediate desegregation, citing potential violence and an untrained staff at the Park Commission and the Memphis Police Department. They proposed a gradual plan of desegregation over a ten-year period. Judge Marion S. Boyd ruled in favor of the City of Memphis and ordered the City to present a plan for full integration to his court within six months.

Attorney A.W. Willis, representing the NAACP, responded, "We always, as a matter of course, appeal cases until they are ruled in our favor or until the court of last resort has ruled." The case was appealed to the United States Court of Appeal Sixth Circuit in Cincinnati, which upheld Judge Boyd's ruling made in Memphis on June 15, 1961.

This ruling prompted the NAACP to file an appeal to the United States Supreme Court. The appeal was made on May 27, 1963. The Supreme Court dealt a fatal blow to segregation in Memphis, ruling that "the Memphis Park Commission was obligated to desegregate all recreational facilities promptly, and further delay would not be permitted."

Following a two-hour meeting between the City Commission and the Memphis Park Commission, a statement was released to the press: "As of today (May 31, 1963), all public recreational facilities operated by the Memphis Park Commission will be operated on a desegregated basis."

For the first time in sixty-three years, African Americans in Memphis could play golf on all City-operated courses without fear of being arrested. For the most part, desegregation went smoothly.

*Dr. Ike A. Watson, Jr. vs The City of Memphis: A New Day: May 27, 1963*

> "Golf was the early battleground of the Civil Rights movement in the United States, along with Voting Rights and equal access to hotels, restaurants, transportation, playgrounds beaches, and other public accommodations."
>
> - George R. Kitsch, Professor History at Manhattan College Riverdale, New York

# TIMELINE OF DESEGREGATION OF MEMPHIS GOLF COURSES

**1960:** Dr. Ike A. Watson Jr. filed a lawsuit in the United States District Court to desegregate golf courses, libraries, museums, all outdoor recreational outlets supported by tax dollars. Attorneys for Dr. Watson were A. W. Willis, Russell Sugarmon, and Ben Hooks.

**1961:** Federal Judge Marion Boyd approved the Memphis Recreational Plan of gradual desegregation. The Memphis Park Commission argued that a gradual plan was needed to avoid violence and general disruption of all recreational programs.

**1961:** The decision was made by plaintiff to appeal the ruling to the United States Six Circuit Court of appeals. On July 7, 1961, the Appeals Court upheld the ruling of Judge Boyd. This meant Memphis would gradually disaggregate its recreational outlets over a period of 10 years.

**1961:** The attorneys for Dr. Ike A. Watson. the plaintiff, appealed to the United States Supreme Court.

**1962:** November 19, 1962, the U.S. Supreme Court agreed to hear the appeal. The case was argued on April 16, 1963.

**1963:** May 27, 1963, the U.S. Supreme Court ruled unanimously for Memphis to properly, desegregate its parks (golf courses included), libraries, and museums, and served notice that southern communities were moving too slowly toward integration of their schools.

The Memphis Plan of gradual desegregation in Memphis was rejected. The court held that the delay violated the constitutional rights of African Americans at the time of the ruling, Pine Hill and Riverside golf courses had been desegregated in 1962.

*First to Tee Off*

**Cleophus Hudson and his Foursome tee off at Pine Hill Golf Course on January 1, 1962. It was a chilly 37 degrees, but Mr. Hudson and his group had a warm feeling on No. 1 tee; they were no longer out of bounds. (The gentleman in the top coat was a reporter for the Memphis World newspaper.)**

Following the 1963 ruling of the U.S. Supreme Court, African Americans were allowed to play on all six city golf courses.

Pleas Jones led a group to Audubon Golf course that included Odessa Dickens, Wade Scott, and Dalton Nickleberry, Sr. As Pleas was unloading his golf bag and strapping it on a pull cart, a white man walked up and kicked the pull cart out of Pleas Jones hand.

Pleas quietly picked up his bag and golf cart and proceeded to the clubhouse. Reflecting on that moment, Pleas said, "If I had done what I wanted to do, it would have been an ugly situation and a negative on the first day we could play on all golf courses." He continued, "I did not want to be a part of anything that reflected negativity on that day."

# RACISM CODIFIED BY THE PROFESSIONAL GOLF ASSOCIATION (PGA) IN 1934

At its annual meeting in 1934, the Professional Golf Association, was the agenda item of defining who could become a member and who could compete in professional golf tournaments in the United States of America.

The PGA was the governing body for all golf pros, the touring pros competing for cash prizes, the club pros who managed golf courses at country clubs and municipal courses. The initial concern was focused on women becoming members of the PGA.

Like a 90-degree turn, the discussion shifted to "Blacks." Do we want Blacks to play and manage the professional game of golf?

Not long after broaching the subject, Section 1, Article III, of the PGA's Constitution and By-laws was adopted to say "Professional golfers of the Caucasian race, over the age of eighteen years, residing in North or South America, and who have served at least five years in the profession (either in the employ of a golf club in the capacity of a professional or in the employ of a professional as his assistant) shall be eligible for membership."

*Dr. L. LaSimba M. Gray, Jr.*

# GOLF WAS THE LAST MAJOR SPORT TO INTEGRATE

## FOOTBALL

**1902:** Charles Follis played with the Shelby Athletic Club.

**1920:** The National Football League was integrated by Fritz Pollard.

**1933:** The National Football League bans African American Players.

**1946:** The NFL team was reintegrated with Kenny Washington and Woody Strode with the Los Angeles Rams.

## BASEBALL

**1947:** In 1947 Jackie Robinson became a Brooklyn Dodger. Jackie would become Rookie of the Year, MVP at his third year.

## BASKETBALL

**1950:** The National Basketball Association breaks the race barrier when Chuck Cooper, Nate Clifton, and Earl Lloyd joined the league.

## GOLF

**1961:** The Professional Golfers Association removes "Caucasian Race" clause from bylaws, opening path for desegregation.

*Out Of Bounds: The History of African Americans and Golf in Memphis*

# AFRICAN AMERICAN PROFESSIONAL GOLFERS WHO CAME TO MEMPHIS

*Dr. L. LaSimba M. Gray, Jr.*

# PHYLLIS G. MEEKINS
# (1927-2005)

Phyllis Meekins was a pioneering African American woman who broke into the ranks of the Ladies Professional Golf Association (LPGA). Her most impressive work was not on the tour but on the driving range and in golf clinics for youth. As her career expanded, the LPGA certified Phyllis as a professional golf instructor.

In 1973, Phyllis established the Phyllis G. Meekins Golf Clinic at Mount Airy's Holy Cross Church in Philadelphia, Pennsylvania.

In 2006, following her death in 2005, the LPGA established the Phyllis G. Meekins Scholarship in her honor, aimed at helping young women of color enjoy golf and pursue college education.

Phyllis joined the legendary Charlie Sifford as guest celebrities for the 1984 Sickle Cell Open at T.O. Fuller Golf Course.

# PETE BROWN
# (1935-2015)

Pete Brown's journey in golf began as a caddy in Jackson, Mississippi. He is best known as the first African American to win on the Professional Golf Association (PGA) Tour with his victory at the Waco Turner Open in 1964.

In 1970, he won the Andy Williams-San Diego Open with an impressive 13 under par, defeating Tony Jacklin in a playoff.

Before joining the PGA Tour, Pete had multiple victories in the United Golfers Association (UGA), including four National Championships, four Lone Star Open Championships, three North and South Championships, and the 1964 Michigan Open. He also tasted victory in Memphis, winning the Rob Wright (T.O. Fuller Open) in 1962.

Pete's story includes his tremendous spirit of winning against great odds. Despite suffering from a non-paralytic form of polio and advised by doctors to give up golf, Pete was determined to return to the tee. His participation in the 1985 Sickle Cell Open was a testament to his resilience.

*Dr. L. LaSimba M. Gray, Jr.*

# CHARLIE SIFFORD
# (1922-2015)

Born in Charlotte, North Carolina, on June 2, 1922, Charlie Sifford began caddying at 13 and by 17, was beating the best golfers in Charlotte. Following the advice of Sutton Alexander, a golf pro at the North Carolina Country Club, Charlie moved to Philadelphia, Pennsylvania, where he found more opportunities to improve his skills.

Charlie faced many hardships in his quest to play on the PGA Tour, enduring life threats and constant harassment. When referred to as the Jackie Robinson of golf, Charlie noted the stark contrast, stating, "Jackie Robinson had eight teammates, hell I'm out here by myself."

In 1960, Charlie became the first African American to receive PGA Approved Tournament Status. He won the Greater Hartford Open in 1967 and the Los Angeles Open in 1969, with several top-ten finishes on the regular tour. In 1975, he won the PGA Seniors Championship and claimed the United Golf Association Championship six times. Reflecting on his late success, Charlie once lamented, "Sometimes I wonder what it could have been like if I could have played the PGA Tour in my prime." His belated honors included induction into the World Golf Hall of Fame in 2004, an Honorary Doctor of Law Degree from the University of St. Andrews in Scotland in 2006, and the renaming of the Revolution Park Golf Course in Charlotte to the Dr. Charles L. Sifford Golf Course in 2011. In 2014, President Barack H. Obama awarded him the Presidential Medal of Freedom.

Despite his many achievements, Charlie Sifford never received an invitation to play in the Masters.

Out Of Bounds: The History of African Americans and Golf in Memphis

*Dr. L. LaSimba M. Gray, Jr.*

# LEE ELDER
## (1934-2021)

Lee Elder was born in Dallas, Texas, in 1934, to the union of Charles and Almeta Elder. He was one of nine children. Tragically, his father was killed in Germany during World War II, and his mother died shortly thereafter.

At the tender age of 12, Lee found himself moving from one relative's house to another, living wherever he was allowed to stay. Eventually, a family decision was made to send him to Los Angeles to live with an aunt.

It was in Los Angeles that Lee learned to caddy to make money. Along with earning a living, he was introduced to golf and life lessons. At 16, he played his first round of 18 holes of golf. He honed his skills and began his stellar career in golf, initially marked by hustling.

After playing a competitive round of golf with Joe Louis, the former Heavyweight Boxing Champion, Lee was introduced to Ted Rhodes, Louis' instructor. Rhodes agreed to teach Lee, and for the next three years, he mentored the young golfer.

Lee Elder earned his PGA Tour Card in 1968 and had an impressive rookie year on the professional tour, winning a total of $38,000. The highlight of his rookie year was a playoff loss to Jack Nicklaus in the American Golf Classic.

In 1974, Lee Elder won the Monsanto Open, earning an invitation to the 1975 Masters. That same year, 1975, Lee Elder came to Memphis to play in the Sickle Cell Open at T.O. Fuller Golf Course.

*Dr. L. LaSimba M. Gray, Jr.*

# TIGER WOODS
## (1975 –)

Out Of Bounds: The History of African Americans and Golf in Memphis

*Dr. L. LaSimba M. Gray, Jr.*

# "TIGER WOODS: THE EPITOME OF DEFIANCE"

*Originally published in The New Tri-State Defender in September 2018.*

**By Dr. L. LaSimba M. Gray, Jr.**

In 1997, shortly after his first Masters Golf Tournament championship, Tiger Woods and his father, Earl Woods, came to Memphis to conduct a clinic at the Pine Hill golf course in South Memphis (not Germantown) for inner-city youth.

I was fortunate to attend the clinic. While most observers were captivated by Tiger's instructions to the youth and the demonstration of his shot making skills, I was awed by the relationship between Tiger and his father.

Earl Woods gave instructions to Tiger in a gentle, yet firm voice: "Tiger, draw the ball. Tiger, fade the ball."

After several amazing golf shots, Earl Woods matter-of-factly said, "Now, drive the green, Tiger."

Tiger asked, "Pop, do you want me to ruin my back?"

Earl Woods was insistent. "Tiger, drive the green."

"OK, Pops."

Tiger pulled a three wood from his bag and swung, seemingly with the greatest of ease. Like a missile, the ball cut through the air and landed on the 17th green. The crowd erupted in cheers and applause.

As I left that clinic, I knew the source of Tiger's greatness. It was the confidence that Earl Woods taught him. "You cannot control what others do, only what you do can you control."

I often wondered how Charles Hudson, the golf pro at Pine Hill, got Tiger Woods to come to Memphis when seemingly other professionals in Memphis could not attract the Tiger.

I later learned that when Tiger first got started, Hudson worked with Earl Woods to financially support Tiger on the tour.

"We sometimes passed the hat to help Tiger with expenses," Hudson recalled.

When I learned of the relationship Hudson had with Tiger and his father, I realized how vital relationships are to meaning in life.

*Out Of Bounds: The History of African Americans and Golf in Memphis*

# PERSPECTIVE

The New Tri-State Defender, September 27 - October 3, 2018, Page 4

**TAKING NOTE!**

## Tiger Woods: The epitome of defiance

*by Dr. L. LaSimba M. Gray Jr.*

In 1997, shortly after his first Masters Golf Tournament championship, Tiger Woods and his father, Earl Woods, came to Memphis to conduct a clinic at the Pine Hill golf course in South Memphis (not Germantown) for inner-city youth.

I was fortunate to attend the clinic. While most observers were captivated by Tiger's instructions to the youth and the demonstration of his shot making skills, I was awed by the relationship between Tiger and his father.

Earl Woods gave instructions to Tiger in a gentle, yet firm voice: "Tiger, draw the ball. Tiger, fade the ball."

After several amazing golf shots, Earl Woods matter-of-factly said, "Now, drive the green, Tiger."

Tiger asked, "Pop, do you want me to run my back?"

Earl Woods was insistent. "Tiger, drive the green."

"OK, Pops."

Tiger pulled a three wood from his bag and swung, seemingly with the greatest of ease. Like a missile, the ball cut through the air and landed on the 17th green. The crowd erupted in cheers and applauses.

As I left that clinic, I knew the source of Tiger's greatness. It was the confidence that Earl Woods taught him. "You cannot control what others do, only what you do can you control."

I often wondered how Charles Hudson, the golf pro at Pine Hill, got Tiger Woods to come to Memphis, when seemingly other professionals in Memphis could not attract the Tiger.

I later learned that when Tiger first got started, Hudson worked with Earl Woods to financially support Tiger on the tour.

"We sometimes passed the hat to help Tiger with expenses," Hudson recalled.

When I learned of the relationship Hudson had with Tiger and his father, I realized how vital relationships are to meaning in life.

The 2019 schedule of professional golf events will bring to Memphis the World Golf Championship, which will be limited to the 50 best players in the world.

Will Tiger Woods show up to play?

For those who say he won't, he couldn't, he ought not to, the Tiger may show up and show out in pure defiance. Last Sunday when Tiger's par putt on the final hole secured victory in the 2018 Tour Championship Golf Tournament in Atlanta, the crowd exploded in praise and appreciation.

There were no fist pumps, neither the trademark uppercuts from Tiger. He majestically – and with obvious emotion – lifted his hands to the sky.

Tiger-mania punctuated all four days of the Tour Championship, spilling an unbelievable swarm of fans onto the final fairway and around the 18th green as it became clear that Woods would win for the first time in five years and notch his 80th professional golf tournament victory. It was the greatest comeback in professional sports.

To really appreciate the significance of victory, one has to know the complete Tiger story, beginning with the facts that he was taught golf by his father, who also taught him how to win. Tiger Woods grew up believing he was a winner, even when the odds were tremendously against him.

Tiger Woods saluted Pine Hill golf course pro Charles Hudson during a Memphis visit in August 1997. (Courtesy photo)

Day 3 of the Tour Championship in Atlanta saw Tiger Woods playing well and a lot of people well, watching. (Photo: Atlanta Voice)

He won his first golf trophy at age 4.

Over the years, his iconic "fist pumps" and his trademark uppercuts were symbolic of the release of pent-up defiance. Tiger Woods had been told by the culture of professional golf, "You can't do this, you can't do that."

The Tiger roar was made to exclaim, "I did it!"

The "fist pump" was in defiance.

Tiger Woods took the golfing world by a storm in 1997. He won his first Masters Championship. He went on to win 14 major championship tournaments and 76 professional golf tournaments. Through 2016, Tiger had won $110 million in tournament play. With endorsements and off-course earnings, he was known as the "Billion Dollar Golfer," having earned an estimated $1.3 billion.

Victory number 80 in Atlanta added an additional $4.62 million.

In 2006, Earl Woods passed away, and Tiger went into deep depression. His mentor, teacher, coach, counselor and guiding force for life was gone. In 2009, the threads of his heroic persona began to unravel. His personal life and marriage became the main menu for tabloids and the media. Many of his sponsors dropped him and some fans withdrew their loyalty. NIKE, however, stood firmly with the champion that lived beneath human frailty.

Throughout his career, Tiger had experienced and endured injuries to his knee, back and ankle. He blew out his knee in the 2008 U. S. Open and in excruciating pain won by 15 strokes. His 79th victory came in 2013, ahead of a series of back surgeries.

In 2014, one week following his back surgery, many observers thought Tiger's career as a professional golfer was over. Professional opinion in the field of chiropractic therapy deemed it impossible for him to return to competitive golf.

The layers of physical and emotional pain, the mounting rise of younger healthier golfers, the increase of glossary, and the loss of his coach and counselor, Tiger Woods had to psychologically revisit his father. He repeated the rich reflections and meditations his father asked him, "Tiger, what did you learn from the negative experience?" That question led Tiger to the resolution of accepting his role in his ways and assuming up to the responsibility of recovery.

Tiger Woods knew at every crises there is a dangerous opportunity, and that he, and he alone, had to rebuild the Tiger brand of greatness. He worked on and off the golf course to defeat the demons within, and the external naysayers, who never gave him a chance of recovery.

At age 42 and with a fused spine, Tiger Woods is again playing golf like no other golfer. He is now dominating.

"I don't know of another golfer who can hit the ball the way I do with a fused spine," he said.

Now methodical in his chipping, consistent with his driver, precise with his irons and deadly with his putter Tiger is back – defiantly!

The 2019 schedule of professional golf events will bring to Memphis the World Golf Championship, which will be limited to the 50 best players in the world.

Will Tiger Woods show up to play?

For those who say he won't, he couldn't, he ought not to, the Tiger may show up and show out in pure defiance. Last Sunday when Tiger's par putt on the final hole secured victory in the 2018 Tour Championship Golf Tournament in Atlanta, the crowd exploded in praise and appreciation.

There were no fist pumps, neither the trademark uppercuts from Tiger. He majestically – and with obvious emotion – lifted his hands to the sky.

Tiger-mania punctuated all four days of the Tour Championship, spilling an unbelievable swarm of fans onto the final fairway and around the 18th green as it became clear that Woods would win for the first time in five years and notch his 80th professional golf tournament victory. It was the greatest comeback in professional sports.

To really appreciate the significance of victory, one has to know the complete Tiger story, beginning with the fact that he was taught golf by his father, who also taught him how to win. Tiger Woods grew up believing he was a winner, even when the odds were tremendously against him. He won his first golf trophy at age 4.

Over the years, his iconic "fist pumps" and his trademark uppercuts were symbolic of the release of pent-up defiance. Tiger Woods had been told by the culture of professional golf, "You can't do this, you can't do that."

The Tiger roar was made to exclaim, "I did it!"

The "fist pump" was in defiance.

Tiger Woods took the golfing world by storm in 1997, when he won his first Masters Championship. He went on to win 14 major championship tournaments and 79 professional golf tournaments. Through 2016, Tiger had won $110 million in tournament play. With endorsements and off-course earnings, he was known as the "Billion Dollar Golfer," having earned an estimated $1.3 billion.

Victory number 80 in Atlanta added an additional $ 4.62 million.

In 2006, Earl Woods passed away, and Tiger went into a deep depression.

His mentor, teacher, coach, counselor and guiding force for life was gone. In 2009, the threads of his heroic person began to unravel. His personal life and marriage became the main menu for tabloids and the media. Many of his sponsors dropped him and some fans withdrew their avidity. NIKE, however, stood firmly with the champion that lived beneath human frailty.

Throughout his career, Tiger had experienced and endured injuries to his knee, back, and ankle. He blew out his knee in the 2000 U.S. Open and in excruciating pain won by 15 strokes. His 79th victory came in 2013, ahead of a series of back surgeries.

In 2014, one week following four back surgeries, many observers thought Tiger's career as a professional golfer was over. Professional opinion in the field of chiropractic therapy deemed it impossible for him to return to competitive golf.

The layers of physical and emotional pain, the increasing rise of younger healthier golfers, the increase of distractors, and the loss of his coach and counselor, Tiger Woods had to psychologically revisit his father. He reported that in his reflections and meditations, his father asked him, "Tiger, what did you learn from the negative experiences?" That question led Tiger to the resolution of accepting his role in his saga and manning up to the responsibility of recovery.

Tiger Woods knew in every crisis there was a dangerous opportunity, and that he, and he alone, had to rebuild the Tiger Woods of greatness. He worked on and off the golf course to defeat the demons within, and the external naysayers, who never gave him a chance of recovery.

At age 42 and with a fused spine, Tiger Woods is again playing golf like no other golfer. He is now dominating.

"I don't know of another golfer who can hit the ball the way I do with a fused spine," he said.

Now methodical in his chipping, consistent with his driver, precise with his irons and deadly with his putter, Tiger is back – defiantly!

Dr. L. LaSimba M. Gray, Jr.

## "TIGER'S GREATEST VICTORY"

*Originally published in The New Tri-State Defender in April 2019.*

**By Dr. L. LaSimba M. Gray, Jr.**

In 1997, the year he won his first professional golf tournament, Tiger Woods also won his first Masters Championship, and he did it in a fashion so dominant that many have long considered it his greatest victory. He set a scoring record of 270 (18 under par), which has stood for the past 22 years (tied by Jordan Spieth in 2015). The margin of victory, 12 strokes, is a record, as is winning at the youngest age, 21.

By raw comparison, Tiger's win Sunday in the 2019 Masters Championship is not only his greatest victory but the greatest comeback victory in professional sports.

Golf is an individual sport and there are no teammates to help you when you fall short. In golf, you play alone and more than the yardage of the course. One has to play the inches between one's ears (golf requires one to think).

To truly appreciate Tiger's greatness, one must know his journey. An observation by Dr. Martin L. King Jr. helps put that journey into context. King said, "The ultimate measure of a man is not where he stands in moments of comfort and convenience, but where he stands at times of challenge and controversy."

Tiger must be measured by the obstacles he has had to overcome in the past 11 years. He has endured injuries to his knee that would have ended the career of an ordinary golfer. He went under the "knife" for back surgery four times. Then he went through the horrific embarrassment of a domestic dispute becoming public.

There was the struggle with pain medication and being falsely arrested for driving under the influence. The public opinion polls turned vicious and mean-spirited. He endured the erosion of his popularity and the increase of naysayers in the worlds of sports and corporate sponsors.

In spite of it all, Tiger Woods is back on top.
African American golfers took great pride when Tiger began to win as a pro and to set records at the Masters Golf Tournament, which stood as the last

*Out Of Bounds: The History of African Americans and Golf in Memphis*

bastion of segregation in professional sports. African Americans were not invited, and corporate sponsors seemingly did not care.

When pressure was applied, the rules to play in the Masters changed and players having won a professional golf tournament the previous year were invited. In 1974, Lee Elder won his first professional golf tournament and was invited to play in th;oe 1975 Masters. Elder was present in 1997 and he, too, thought Tiger's victory was the greatest.

In 1997, Tiger was just starting out as a professional golfer. He was young, strong and filled with confidence. The legendary Jack Nicklaus predicted that year that Tiger would become one of the greatest to ever play the game. In 1997, Tiger had his father, Earl Woods, to keep him focused. In 1997, corporate sponsors were lined up to place Tiger Woods on the brand of products and services.

As 2019 unfolded, it was still being debated as to whether Tiger could win another major golf tournament. In a real metaphorical sense, Tiger was on an endangered list. Golfing analysts readily talked about how great he once was in years gone by and cast serious doubts as to whether he could return to greatness.

Phil Mickleson, a fellow Master's Tournament champion, took a different view: "Tiger doesn't need golf, golf needs Tiger."

*Tiger Woods (center, in gray) brought youth, expertise, skill and excitement to The Masters -- and African American interest in the sport skyrocketed.*

When Tiger teed off for the final round of the 2019 Masters, he trailed the leader by two strokes. When he reached the 18th hole, he had a two-stroke cushion. This meant he had two putts to win his fifth green jacket, two putts to win his 15th major golf tournament, two putts to win his 81st professional golf tournament and two putts to win $2,000,070. More importantly, he had two strokes to regain the "Throne of Greatness" in professional golf.

In 1997, Earl Woods was there to greet his son and celebrate the momentous Master's Tournament victory. In 2019, little Charlie Woods was there to meet Tiger, his daddy, and celebrate his father's greatest victory. It was difficult to find a person with dry eyes in the gallery.

Out Of Bounds: The History of African Americans and Golf in Memphis

# PERSPECTIVE

The New Tri-State Defender, April 18 - 24, 2019, Page 4

Following the Masters win President Donald Trump tweeted "Spoke to Tiger Woods to congratulate him on the great victory he had in yesterday's TheMasters, & to inform him that because of his incredible Success & Comeback in Sports (Golf) and, more importantly, LIFE, I will be presenting him with the PRESIDENTIAL MEDAL OF FREEDOM!"

# Tiger's greatest victory

by Dr. L. LaSimba M. Gray Jr.
Special to The New Tri-State Defender

In 1997, the year he won his first professional golf tournament, Tiger Woods also won his first Masters Championship and he did it in a fashion so dominant that many have long considered it his greatest victory. He set a scoring record of 270 (18 under par), which has stood for the past 22 years (tied by Jordan Spieth in 2015.) The margin of victory, 12 strokes, is a record, as is winning at the youngest age, 21.

By raw comparison, Tiger's win Sunday in the 2019 Masters Championship is not only his greatest victory but the greatest comeback victory in professional sports.

Golf is an individual sport and there are no teammates to help you when you fall short. In golf, you play alone and more than the yardage of the course. One has to play the inches between one's ears (golf requires one to think).

To truly appreciate Tiger's greatness, one must know his journey. An observation by Dr. Martin L. King Jr. helps put that journey into context. King said, "the ultimate measure of a man is not where he stands in moments of comfort and convenience, but where he stands in times of challenge and controversy."

Tiger must be measured by the obstacles he has had to overcome in the past 14 years. He has endured injuries to his knee that would have ended the career of an ordinary golfer. He went under the "knife" for back surgery four times. Then he went through the horrific embarrassment of a domestic dispute becoming public.

There was the struggle with pain medication and being falsely arrested for driving under the influence. The public opinion polls turned vicious and mean-spirited. He endured the erosion of his popularity and the insurance of naysayers in the worlds of sports and corporate sponsors.

In spite of it all, Tiger Woods is back on top.

African-American golfers took great pride when Tiger began to win as a pro and to set records at the Masters Golf Tournament, which stood as the last bastion of segregation in professional sports. African Americans were not invited and corporate sponsors seemingly did not care.

Dr. L. LaSimba M. Gray Jr.

When pressure was applied, the rules to play in the Masters changed and players having won a major professional golf tournament the previous year were invited. In 1974, Lee Elder won his first professional golf tournament and was invited to play in the 1975 Masters. Elder was present in 1997 and he, too, thought Tiger's victory was the greatest.

In 1997, Tiger was just starting out as a professional golfer. He was young, strong and filled with confidence. The legendary Jack Nicklaus predicted that year that Tiger would become one of the greatest to ever play the game. In 1997, Tiger had his father, Earl Woods, to keep him focused. In 1997, corporate sponsors were lined up to place Tiger Woods on the board of products and services.

As 2019 unfolded, it was still being debated as to whether Tiger could win another major golf tournament. In a real metaphorical sense, Tiger was on an endangered list. Golfing analysts readily talked about how great he once was in years gone by and cast serious doubts as to whether he could return to greatness.

Phil Mickelson, a fellow Master's Tournament champion, took a different view: "Tiger doesn't need golf, golf needs Tiger."

When Tiger teed off for the final round of the 2019 Masters, he trailed the leader by two strokes. When he reached the 18th hole, he had a two-stroke cushion. This means he had two putts to win his fifth green jacket, two putts to win his 15th major golf tournament, two putts to win his 81st professional golf tournament and two putts to win $2,000,070.

More importantly, he had two strokes to regain the "Throne of Greatness" in professional golf.

In 1997, Earl Woods was there to greet his son and celebrate the momentous Master's Tournament victory. In 2019, little Charlie Woods was there to meet Tiger, his daddy, and celebrate his father's greatest victory. It was difficult to find a person with dry eyes in the gallery.

*Dr. L. LaSimba M. Gray, Jr.*

## **WHERE IS THE NEXT TIGER WOODS?**

How close are we to seeing the next Tiger Woods?
"The main thing that's missing from young African American players is training. We need some kind of training around that will support minority golfers who want to take their games to the next level."
— Lee Elder

"We all know the systematic problems of racism and white supremacy. What is the solution? How do we move the needle?"

*Out Of Bounds: The History of African Americans and Golf in Memphis*

# J.P. THORNTON

J.P. Thornton's story is a classic Memphis tale of grit and grind on the golf course. From the get-go, his path wasn't your typical straight shot down the fairway.

Starting out at The Links at Pine Hill, moving through an impressive run at White Station High and Texas Southern College, to navigating the tough road of professional golf, Thornton's journey is all about perseverance and passion.

Born in 1985, Thornton's not slowing down; he's just getting started. After years of juggling day jobs with his golf dreams, playing on developmental and mini tours, he's making moves. Winning his first APGA Tour event at TPC Sugarloaf in Atlanta was a game-changer, landing him a sponsorship deal with Veritex Bank and setting his sights on the Korn Ferry Tour Qualifying School.

Lately, he's taking a swing at something new, too—broadcasting. Known for his big personality, he's stepping into the booth as an in-studio analyst for PGA Tour Live. It's a new challenge, but he's ready for it, bringing his trademark smile and humor to the screen.

Life threw Thornton a curveball with the loss of his firstborn, leading him to step back from golf. But with the support of his wife and the joy of his daughter, he found his way back to the game. Now, with golf as his full-time job, he's aiming to make it on the Korn Ferry Tour and maybe even find a future in broadcasting.

Above all, Thornton wants to give back, to open doors for kids in Memphis like those opened for him. It's about more than golf; it's about inspiring others to chase their dreams, just like he did.

"I want to pay it forward," he told *The Commercial Appeal* in 2021. "I want to help provide opportunities to other kids and expose them to the game. I want to inspire other people to pursue their dreams and just do what God puts on your heart."

## Out Of Bounds: The History of African Americans and Golf in Memphis

*A young J.P. Thornton earlier in his career and still loving the game as an adult.*

Dr. L. LaSimba M. Gray, Jr.

# BRIA SANDERS

In the storied fairways of Memphis, where the spirit of competition and the pursuit of excellence have long intertwined, Bria Sanders emerges as a beacon of youthful determination and unwavering ambition.

Born with the game coursing through her veins, Sanders, a proud product of Cordova, TN, set her sights on the lush greens and challenging bunkers of golf from a tender age. By the age of 15, her commitment to the sport was undeniable, dedicating herself to rigorous practice sessions and competitive play, embodying the Memphis ethos.

Sanders' journey through the ranks of junior golf was marked by a string of impressive achievements, including showing her stuff at International Junior Golf Tour events, where she not only competed but triumphed, securing victories that heralded her arrival on the national stage. Ranked 87th nationally among junior girls, her performances were a testament to her skill, dedication, and the competitive spirit fostered in the heart of Memphis.

The collegiate greens beckoned, and Sanders answered the call with aplomb. As a testament to her enduring dedication and skill, she was recognized among Golfstat's Top 50 NAIA Women's Golfers, a distinction that spoke volumes of her growth and her relentless pursuit of excellence. Her journey from the nurturing grounds of Memphis to the collegiate arenas, and her aspirations for the professional stage, encapsulate not just the story of a golfer, but the enduring spirit of Memphis itself—a city that breeds champions, nurtures dreams, and celebrates the relentless pursuit of greatness.

*Golf professional Loren Roberts teaches the swing to a young Bria Sanders.*

Out Of Bounds: The History of African Americans and Golf in Memphis

Thank you Mr. Charles for helping me
Bria' Sand

*Dr. L. LaSimba M. Gray, Jr.*

# DOMINANT PERSONALITIES OF AFRICAN AMERICAN GOLFERS IN MEMPHIS

### AFRICAN AMERICAN WOMEN GOLFERS

Odessa Dickens, Annie Green, Bria Sanders, Amanda Tibbs, Florence Scott, Lillian Crockett McCray, Millicent Bolton, Erma Laws, Connie Spruell, Katherine Bennett, and Judge Earnestine Hunt Dorse were all prominent figures in the world of golf.

Carrie Jones, although not a Memphis resident, had a stellar career in amateur golf that spanned over five decades in Memphis and the Greater Mid-South. Her winning streak began in Memphis in 1962, where she won the Women's Division of the United Golfers Association National Championship at T.O. Fuller Golf Course.

Jones relished the competition and fellowship of Memphians, as well as the challenges posed by Memphis city golf courses. Her rivalry with Odessa Dickens of Memphis was particularly notable, with the two often battling for the championship in local tournaments. Carrie, along with her husband Sam Jones, frequently traveled to Memphis to support clubs and charitable golf tournaments. She won the Sickle Cell Open on numerous occasions and was always considered the favorite to win in any tournament she entered.

In 2016, the Women for Progress of Mississippi organized the First Carrie Jones Golf Classic at the Canton Country Club in Canton, Mississippi. The mission of this Classic is to support women in golf, continuing the legacy of Carrie Jones and her contributions to the sport.

*Out Of Bounds: The History of African Americans and Golf in Memphis*

*Above: Odessa Dickens was known as an avid golfer and also for her fashion sense. She was always among the best dressed golfers in Memphis.*

*Left: Annie Green was seen at all of the tournaments and was a frequent participant in many of them. She loved to be around the game.*

*Dr. L. LaSimba M. Gray, Jr.*

**MISCONCEPTION LEADS TO DEFEAT**

In the fall of 2022, I visited an auto broker in Marion, Arkansas, named Kent Hallum. While sitting in the waiting area, I noticed a poster from the Masters Golf Tournament.

Curious, I inquired, "What year is this?" He proudly cited the year and asked if I played golf. My affirmative response led to a 15-minute discussion about local and national golf, golf clubs, and the hustling game of Memphis and the Mid-South. He was a member of Meadowbrook Country Club in West Memphis and very graciously invited me over for a round of golf.

Hallum had fallen victim to the practice of inviting guest golfers to play against a home team at their chosen course. The home team consisted of young, energetic professionals, while the visiting team was composed of a senior player and a cross-handed hitter.

Then he shifted gears, "Do you know a golfer with the Memphis School System who plays cross-handed?" I responded, "I know Donald Holmes very well." "And the old man he plays with?" "I know Thurman Glass as well."

Hallum continued with a mix of laughter and excitement.

"I invited Donald Holmes over for a round to play my hand-picked team and told Don he could bring anybody he wanted. When I saw them approach the practice area, I thought to myself, there's no way they can beat my team of young, strong professionals. I gladly covered the bet."

Curious, I asked, "How did you come out?"

"We lost the match but found new friends on the golf course," he replied. "I learned a very expensive lesson: perceptions can be deceiving."

What Kent Hallum did not know was the winning history of this touring team of golfing legends. Donald Holmes has been winning golf matches and tournaments since he was a teenager in the 1970s, and Thurman Glass has a record of consistent wins beginning in 1962.

My maternal grandmother, Armentha Phillips, would often say, "You can't judge a book by its cover."

*Dr. L. LaSimba M. Gray, Jr.*

# THE MEMPHIS SICKLE CELL ANEMIA OPEN CHARITY GOLF TOURNAMENT

*Out Of Bounds: The History of African Americans and Golf in Memphis*

*Dr. L. LaSimba M. Gray, Jr.*

# THE SICKLE CELL OPEN

All news outlets covered the tournament extensively, and word-of-mouth sharing by golfers made the Sickle Cell Open the number one amateur golf tournament for African Americans in the Greater Mid-South.

Following the 1974 tournament, Walter Evans and Leon Griffin joined the Board of Directors, specifically working with the golf tournament. These upstanding socialites were members of the 19th Holers, a prominent golf club for African Americans. The 19th Holers traditionally held their annual golf tournament on Labor Day weekend at T.O. Fuller Golf Course.

Sam Qualls, president of the 19th Holers, attended the planning meeting for the 1976 Sickle Cell Open and generously offered to surrender their spot on the T.O. Fuller calendar to the Sickle Cell Open. This gesture was received with great enthusiasm by Johnny Arnold and Miller Brewing Company.

In the inaugural tournament in 1973, there were 151 entrants. By 1974, the number had grown to 205, and in 1975 and 1976, there were 150 entrants, making the Sickle Cell Open the largest amateur golf tournament for African Americans in Memphis and the Greater Mid-South.

For the 1976 tournament, efforts were made to enhance its appeal. Hostesses were added, each foursome was provided with scorers, and the awards ceremony featured the previous winner presenting a Green Jacket to the new champion. The award ceremony, held at the 18th hole green, became the highlight of every tournament.

Out Of Bounds: The History of African Americans and Golf in Memphis

*Dr. Gray, along with Jim "Mudcat" Grant and Tommy Davis. Raymond Tate is standing.*

## WINNERS OF THE GREEN JACKET:

Walter Anderson

Pleas Jones

Thurman Glass

Donald Holmes

Mason West, Sr.

Elton Granbury, Sr.

Robert Dolman

Dalton Nickleberry, Jr.

*Dr. L. LaSimba M. Gray, Jr.*

*Calvin Vinson, Donald Holmes, Thurman Glass and Dr. Gray.*

## THE GREEN JACKET AND BLACK GOLF

The Sickle Cell America Golf Tournament was organized in 1973 by Dr. L. LaSimba M. Gray, Jr., Executive Director of the Memphis Regional Sickle Cell America Council, Inc. In its first year, the tournament achieved such success that Johnny Arnold of Arnold and Associates secured Miller Brewing as a major sponsor for the 1974 tournament.

Mr. Arnold managed all the promotional publicity and post-tournament press releases. His personal connection to the cause was profound, as he had a son, "Twiffy," who suffered from sickle cell anemia. He was assisted in his efforts by William "Bill" Adkins and Linda Elmore Adkins.

## From the Founder—President

Dear Supporter,

The Memphis Regional Sickle Cell Council is a non-profit organization involved in the war against Sickle Cell Anemia and the many implications thereof.

The Council is made up of the greatest cross-section of the Memphis community, the members are Black and White, conservative and liberal, rich and poor, patient and impatient, but all working for a common goal. That goal is to assemble and disseminate information to increase the awareness of the problems inherent in Sickle Cell Anemia; the expansion of detection services; to assure the adequate referral facilities are available to care for persons identified as having Sickle Cell Anemia; to provide adequate counseling (informative, not advisory) to persons identified as anemia or trait carriers; to promote optimal rehabilitative (resources) for Sickle Cell patient; the encouragement and promotion of further research into the problems of Sickle Cell Anemia; to solicit funds as may be necessary, from local, state and federal agencies and private sources.

The Memphis Regional Sickle Cell Council has been organized to advocate for the support the grassroot's vanguard in the fight to eradicate Sickle Cell Anemia. It offers a community united front against a tragic blood disorder which threatens the health of our community.

The Memphis Regional Sickle Cell Council offers the following services: public education, tutorial services, screening (testing for detection), counseling, patient rehabilitation and care and social services. These services are supported by proceeds from the Annual Golf Tournament, contracts and private donations.

We are deeply grateful to you for your continued support.

Sincerely,

Leo M. Gray, Jr.
Executive Director

**MEMPHIS REGIONAL SICKLE CELL COUNCIL, INC.**
**STAFF MEMBERS**
**FY 82-83**

L to R: Patrisha A. Jackson, Administrative Asst.; Leo M. Gray, Jr. Executive Dir.; Teresa R. Freeman, Fiscal Officer; Regina Mottley, Phlebotomist; Ajaners Williams, Genetic Counselor; Harvey Tharp, Educatioanal Coordinator; Marjorie Mayhue, Regional SSI Manager; Mildred B. Hunter, Phlebotomist Asst.

**SCOREKEEPER/HOSTESSES**
**11th ANNUAL GOLF TOURNEY**

1st Row L to R: Teresa Washington, Barbara Mosley, Vivian Crawford, Mercury Bowie, Maxine Johnson, Pat Handy and Walter Evans, Tourney Dir. 2nd Row L to R: Bernie Stevens, Mattie Parker, Annette Fields, Mary Johnson and Pat Jackson. 3rd Row L to R: Helen Payne, Diane White, Ruthie Austin, Deloris Cheatham, and Annette Garner.

*Dr. L. LaSimba M. Gray, Jr.*

## From the President

Welcome to the 11th Annual Sickle Cell Benefit Golf Tournament and to the City of Memphis. I would like to express, on behalf of the Memphis Regional Sickle Cell Council, my heart-felt gratitude to each of you for supporting this cause. Realizing the individual sacrifices each of you made, it is even more heart warming. It's also encouraging to know that the ranks are now being filled to wage an effective war - Against Sickle Cell Anemia. There is no need to draft you, for your presence and support indicate your volunteered dedication.

Our special thanks to our Sponsors WKDJ, WHRK, Universal Life Insurance and Federal Express, merchants and Mr. Lee Elder for prizes and all that makes this the greatest Amateur Goll Tournament in the city.

I sincerely trust that you will have an eventful and most enjoyable tournament and stay in Memphis.

Gratefully yours,

Dr. J.W. Westbrook, Chairman
Board of Directors
MRSCC, Inc.

## The Directors Speaks

I sincerely wish to express appreciation to all participants and a special appreciation to WKDJ radio 680 and WHRK-97 and the General Tournament Committee for making it possible that I extend you a hearty welcome.

If by any measure this project is a success, it will be because of the tremendous support received from dedicated members of our community, interest, and support from our visiting friends and supporters.

We owe a special thanks to Mr. Lee Elder.

Respectfully,

Walter Evans
Tournament Director

*Out Of Bounds: The History of African Americans and Golf in Memphis*

## UNIVERSAL Life Insurance Company

HOME OFFICE 480 LINDEN AVENUE AT DANNY THOMAS BOULEVARD
MEMPHIS, TENNESSEE 38126 — P.O. BOX 241

**"A Good Place to Buy Life Insurance... And a Good Place to Work"**

Operating area: Arkansas, California, Kansas, Louisiana, Mississippi, Missouri, Tennessee, Oklahoma, Texas, Virginia, and the District of Columbia.

705 S. PARKWAY E.
MEMPHIS, TENNESSEE
L. O. TAYLOR, MANAGER

119 S. 12th STREET
WEST MEMPHIS, ARKANSAS
J. W. McKINNEY, MANAGER

Thurman Glass shot a 138 and Carrie Jones shot a 159.

*Dr. L. LaSimba M. Gray, Jr.*

# WKDJ-WHRK AIR PERSONALITIES

## ANNUAL SICKLE CELL TOURNAMENT

### FACT SHEET
### OPEN AMATEUR
### 36 HOLES MEDAL PLAY

| YEAR | NO. OF ENTRANTS | WINNER | WINNING SCORE |
| --- | --- | --- | --- |
| 1973 | 137 | Pleas Jones | -6 |
| 1974 | 205 | Thurman Glass | -6 |
| 1975 | 150 | Mason West | -6 |
| 1976 | 150 | Walter Anderson | -7 |
| 1977 | 150 | Pleas Jones | -3 |
| 1978 | 147 | Thurman Glass | -3 |
| 1979 | 151 | Alvin Starks | -3 |
| 1980 | 164 | Walter Anderson | -11 |
| 1981 | 157 | Donald Holmes | -2 |
| 1982 | 157 | Thurman Glass | -4 |
| 1983 | 197 | Walter Anderson | -9 |
| 1984 | 187 | Donald Holmes | -7 |
| 1985 | 167 | Thurman Glass | -12 ** |
| 1986 | 129 | Thurman Glass | -11 |
| 1987 | 166 | Donald Holmes | -4 |
| 1988 | 160 | Donald Holmes | -5 |
| 1989 | 144 | Donald Holmes | -2 |
| 1990 | 140 | Donald Holmes | -5 |
| 1991 | 136 | Donald Holmes | -4 |
| 1992 | 120 | Donald Holmes | -4 |
| 1993 | 130 | Jerry Butler | -4 |
| 1994 | 120 | Donald Holmes | -6 |
| 1995 | 128 | Donald Holmes | -4 |
| 1996 | 129 | Donald Holmes | -4 |
| 1997 | 144 | Randy Perry | E |

*This fact sheet shows the history of the Sickle Cell Golf Tournament.*

*Dr. L. LaSimba M. Gray, Jr.*

# TRIBUTES TO TRUE GOLFING LEGENDS

Lillie McCray (L) receives the Ladies Publinks trophy from Galloway G.C. Facility Manager Mickey Barker.

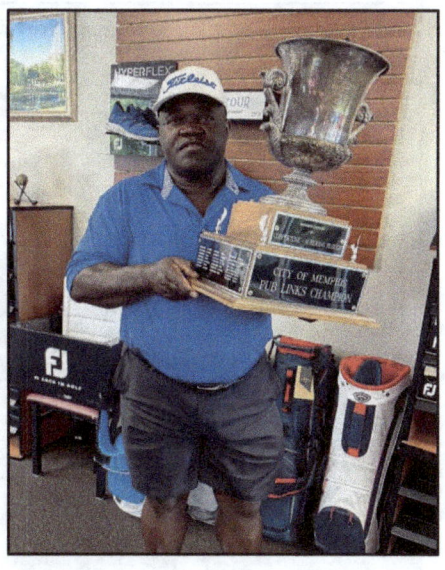

Lillie McCray is a force on the course and so is her husband Polk. Together they are a power couple of Memphis Golf.

## POWER COUPLE OF MEMPHIS GOLF
### Polk and Lillie McCray

Polk McCray's foray into the world of golf began in the ranks of caddies at Ridgeway Country Club in Collierville, Tennessee.

Mr. Esau Johnson would drive through the African American community, picking up young men eager to work at the Country Club as caddies. Polk McCray joined this group, initially to make money, but soon realized it was the beginning of a new journey in life.

Beyond earning money, he was exposed to golf, which became a life-changer for him. Polk became the first African American to play on the golf team at Collierville High School, continuing his caddying at Ridgeway and playing the course on Mondays.

His journey at Ridgeway started in 1976, and twenty years later, Polk was crowned champion of the 1996 Memphis Publinx Golf Tournament. The Memphis Publinx Tournament, the crown jewel of amateur golf in Memphis, brought his name to the forefront of golfing conversations at T.O. Fuller and Pine Hill. Questions like "Who is he?" "Where did he come from?" and "Have you seen him play?" buzzed in the golfing culture, previously familiar only with names like Elton Grandberry, Mason West,

Dr. L. LaSimba M. Gray, Jr.

*Polk McCray's game earned him regular coverage in media.*

Local Publinks legend, Polk McCray, gives his wife Lillie some quality advice on her putting line at the 2007 Memphis Ladies Publinks Championship.

Walter Anderson, Charlie Wilson, Don Holmes, Pleas Jones, and Thurman Glass. Polk McCray's emergence led to a growing fan base eager to watch and cheer for this new golfing phenomenon. He went on to win the Memphis Publinx four additional times in 1999, 2000, 2001, and 2009.

In 1997, a corporate transfer brought a significant change in Polk's life. Lillian Crockett was transferred to Memphis by Standard Registers Corporation. She discovered Pine Hill Golf Course and met her future coach, caddie, and husband, Polk McCray. They began playing golf together, and in 2004, they took their relationship to the next level by getting married.

Lillian had learned to play golf in Dayton, Ohio, at the Madden Golf Course under the legendary Pete Brown, the club professional and instructor. Pete, the first African American to win a PGA-sponsored tournament, played on both the regular PGA and Senior tours but had a great passion for teaching golf to the next generation. Lillian was one of his best students.

Together, the McCrays pursued their passion for golf. Mrs. Lillian McCray became a force to be reckoned with in 1999, winning in the Ladies' division of the Memphis Publinx Tournament. She won numerous

*Polk McCray (right) with some of his competitors at Memphis Publinx.*

tournaments across the country, but when asked about her greatest achievement, she would readily respond, "The five times I won the Women's Championship in the Memphis Publinx Tournament."

Now retired, the McCrays enjoy regular rounds of golf at the Galloway Golf Course. In addition to caddying for each other, Polk also serves as a caddie on the Korn Ferry Tour.

*Dr. L. LaSimba M. Gray, Jr.*

*Marie Nugent, Charlie Wilson and the Author, Dr. LaSimba Gray.*

# CHARLIE WILSON

Charlie Wilson earned many nicknames of endearment: "Pie Kid," "Pie," "Sweet Swing," "Light Gravy," and "Charlie Tuna." The above nicknames were used with the utmost respect in conversations about Charlie Wilson.

Charlie was born on July 12, 1924, to his beloved mother, Josephine Wilson. His birth positioned him to be the second son of three sons. Charlie Wilson grew up in a segregated Memphis in the Binghampton Community, in the shadows of the Chickasaw Country Club.

It was at Chickasaw Country Club that Charlie learned the game of golf as a caddie. The older caddies taught the younger caddies the game of golf on "Mondays," when a Negro Caddy could play the golf course. Charlie was an excellent student and soon discovered he could beat all the caddies and most of the professionals at Chickasaw Country Club.

Charlie had great potential but also a great handicap: he was a "Negro." Negroes were not allowed to play professional golf. Charlie Wilson was a very confident person who knew himself in the context of a segregated society. He was defined from within, and he allowed the external to roll off [his back] like water off a duck's back.

Charlie Wilson was quiet and resolved. He knew something had to be done about the wrongs of a segregated park system that denied African Americans the opportunity to play public golf courses. Charlie joined a city-wide protest against the Memphis Park Commission for not providing golf courses for African Americans equal to "White only" Golf courses funded by tax dollars. This protest led to the establishment of the First Golf nine-hole Course built for "Negroes" in Memphis. The Douglas Park Golf Course was the site for many African Americans to learn the game of golf.

Charlie's reputation grew rapidly in the greater mid-south when he and local golfers began to travel the Negro Golfing "Chitlin's Circuit." He was always a gentleman, soft-spoken, and willing to share golfing techniques and wisdom.

Charlie became a favorite in Mobile, Alabama; Little Rock, Arkansas; St. Louis, Missouri; Atlanta, Georgia; Jackson, Mississippi; Birmingham, Alabama; and Bowling Green, Kentucky. He easily won the hearts of aspiring young golfers across the nation.

In Memphis, he joined the original board of directors of the First Tee of Memphis and worked closely with Charles Hudson and Calvin Vinson to teach urban youth the challenging game of golf. Many of his former students are now productive citizens, in many walks of life, making Charlie Wilson proud every step of the way.

In 2011, on the first Wednesday of April, Charlie Wilson walked onto the Augusta National Golf Course. This was a lifelong dream of Charlie to go to the Masters. Members of New Sardis, students, and golfing buddies of Charlie Wilson, put our nickels together and rented a luxury Escalade Cadillac, secured three tickets for admission, and made hotel reservations in Augusta, GA.

Pastor Dr. L. LaSimba M. Gray Jr., Rev. John Glaze, and Charlie loaded up Tuesday morning and hit the highway. This trip was made possible through the generosity of appreciative members and friends of Charlie Wilson. Charlie Wilson did not have to spend a dime; everything was paid for from donations.

Charlie wanted to sit at the turn; through his golf course wisdom, he said, "Pastor, if I sit here at the turn, I can see all the pros."

The Sunday, following the trip to the Masters, Charlie Wilson received his green jacket for having gone to the Masters. His response: "Thank you one and all."

Charlie was a faithful member of New Sardis Historical Baptist Church in Germantown, Tennessee, where he served as an usher. During the golfing season, he could be found most Saturday mornings on the Charlie Wilson Driving Range on the church campus. He volunteered at Highland Oaks Elementary School as a fatherly mentor for children without a father in the home. Charlie never missed a "Dads and Doughnuts Program."

Charlie was a distinguished and reserved member of the Par Makers Golf Club of Bowling Green, Kentucky. Despite facing segregation and limited opportunities, Charlie's passion and skill in golf, coupled with his commitment to his community, left a lasting legacy. During the Living Legends Celebration of African American History in 2014, Charlie "Sweet Swing" Wilson was honored for his numerous contributions to golf in Memphis. He was both loved and respected by the participants. Charlie Wilson "received his flowers" at New Sardis Baptist Church after attending the Masters in 2014.

*Willie and Cornelius Burkins were avid golfers -- and professional golf club makers.*

# BURKINS BROTHERS: PROFESSIONAL CLUBMAKERS

Willie and Cornelius Burkins were attracted to golf in efforts to make money. They would caddie at the Colonial Country Club and ended up at the Bert Dargie Golf Company, making golf clubs.

The Bert Dargie Golf Company was founded by Scottish immigrants in 1908. The company was best known for its custom golf club manufacturing. Bert Dargie III, started out early in life as an apprentice to his father and grandfather in the business and, at age 15, was considered a master craftsman. The Dargie Golf Company was frequently visited by touring PGA Legends including Arnold Palmer, Fuzzy Zoeller, Lee Trevino, Tom Kite, and Chi Chi Rodriguez. Golf clubs made by the Dargie Golf Company were shipped all over the world.

Willie and Cornelius Burkins were joined by their cousin, Dave Alexander, at the Dargie Company. Because of the high demands for the Dargie Golf Clubs, Willie, Cornelius, and Dave were trained to duplicate the skills of Bert Dargie III. They did that, to the mentoring satisfaction of Bert Dargie and the company. All three of these African Americans became master craftsmen in golf club manufacturing and repair.

The Bert Dargie Golf Company was negatively impacted when the golf industry switched from wood-headed clubs to metal. Bert Dargie's specialty was the persimmon-headed clubs.

*"It don't mean a thing if it ain't got that swing."* — Duke Ellington

The lyrics of Duke Ellington's mega-hit of the swing era may not have directly applied to golf, but many African American players practiced getting that ideal swing of the golf club. The standard setters were Teddy Rhodes, Bill Spiller, Charlie Sifford, and Pete Bowman.

Locally, golfers like Charlie Wilson, Pleas Jones, Thurman Glass, and Cornelius Burkins, "Sho nuff" had that swing.

#1 Willie Burkins started working at Bert Dargie in 1955 and Cornelius joined in 1961. Their cousin Dave Alexander would join the team later.

*Cornelius Burkins takes a swing.*
*The swing means everything in golf!*

#2 Willie and Cornelius Burkins became addicted to golf and built their own sandlot course in the White Station area. The course consisted of two holes where the Home Depot (at Poplar and Truse Parkway) is now located.

"We used a sling blade, hoes, and shovels to clear the ground," said Cornelius. "It was hard work, but we wanted to play and that was our course."

Willie and Cornelius Burkins became respected golfers on the African American Chitlin' Circuit. Dave played a little golf, but his passion was making and repairing golf clubs. Cornelius, commenting on the skills of Dave Alexander, said, "He was a fair golfer but one helluva club maker."

Cornelius Burkins is the present-day guru on African Americans in

*Cornelius Burkins in his shop applying the craft of golf-club manufacturing.*

Memphis Golf. He has a long tenure in the African American fraternity of Golf and holds the self-gratification of six holes in one, countless trophies, and memories to the infinite power.

*Dr. L. LaSimba M. Gray, Jr.*

*Often referred to as "The Black Jack Nicklaus," Ted Rhodes won more than 150 tournaments in his career, but never got to compete against his white counterparts in the PGA. (By Golf Legacy - Own work, CC BY-SA 4.0, https://commons.wikimedia.org/w/index) php?curid=98605283)*

# THEODORE "TED" RHODES
# (1913-1969)

Theodore "Ted" Rhodes was born in Nashville, Tennessee, where he developed a habit-like interest in golf. As a young man, he began to caddie at the Belle Meade and Richland Country Clubs.

Rhodes joined the U.S. Navy during World War II, and following his discharge, made a commitment to play professional golf. He enjoyed the flare of flashy clothes, the applause and cheers of the crowd, and ultimately the thrill of victory. His biggest handicap was his ethnicity: he was Black.

Ted Rhodes emerged as the King of the golf circuit of the United Golfers Association. This organization was the alternative to the PGA, which dismissed African American golfers' participation in their tournaments and profession.

In 1948, with the support of Joe Louis and the NAACP, Ted Rhodes filed a lawsuit against the PGA for its codified discrimination: the "Caucasian only Clause" for membership. The suit was settled out of court, allowing the PGA to shift its base of discrimination from race to invitational-sponsored tournaments. Participation in golf tournaments by qualification is purely objective, whereas participation by invitation is purely subjective.

Ted Rhodes had won over 150 times on the UGA Circuit. He was eager to demonstrate his skills on a bigger stage: the PGA Tour.

In a strategy orchestrated by Joe Louis, the PGA was embarrassed in the court of public opinion when the great Heavyweight Boxing champion and a veteran of World War II was denied participation in the 1952 San Diego Open Invitational. Louis had been invited, but President Horton was reminded of the Caucasian-only rule, and Louis was not allowed to play.

Joe Louis arrived at the San Diego Country Club at 7:00 am to qualify, intending to force the PGA to publicly deny his participation solely based on his race. Joe Louis lamented, "We've got other hills to get by."

He was in the struggle to rid the PGA of its "Caucasian only Clause" with a new resolve.

"I didn't expect they'd let me play when I came down here," he reflected, "But I wanted 'em to tell me personally. I wanted to bring this thing out into the light, so the people can know what the PGA is."

Ted Rhodes wanted to compete on the PGA Tour during his prime. Time was running out, and after a round of 33 on the nine-hole Cumberland Golf Course in Nashville, Theodore "Ted" Rhodes passed away from a heart attack. (Maybe a broken heart).

The eulogy by Charlie Sifford: "He was the Black Jack Nicklaus, but you've probably never heard of him because he was Black and living at the wrong time. His story is one of the great tragedies of Golf."

Ted Rhodes was a young 55 when he made his transition. Maggie Hathaway, of the Los Angeles Sentinel, wrote, "Hope you enjoy the heavenly courses where all golfers are equal."

## THURMAN "DUNNA" GLASS

While very few people in the Memphis Golfing Culture know Thurman's nickname as "Dunna", he could just as fittingly have been called "Smooth" due to his personality and style of play. He is always as smooth as glass.

Thurman studied the game of golf through intense observation. He watched the players and professionals at Colonial Country Club through the fence and then spent hours with his golf clubs trying to duplicate what he had seen. Thurman is a rarity for his era of golf; he did not caddy, as most African Americans did, to find a way into golf.

Thurman's interest in golf led him to join Cornelius and Willie Burkins in building a sandlot golf course in the White Station section of Memphis. Cornelius Burkins reported, "We used swing blades and push lawnmowers to cut the grass and make our holes."

Family and friends made up the gallery and encouraged the competition. In a habit-like fashion, Thurman pursued golf and emerged as a frequent winner in the Memphis world of amateur golf. He won his first tournament in 1962, the Sam Quarles Tournament at T.O. Fuller Golf Course.

He would go on to win the Ted Rhodes Tournament in Nashville three times, an extraordinary feat considering this was the World Series for African American golfers in the nation. Thurman won the Memphis Publinks Tournament twice, in 1976 and 1981, and the Memphis Senior Publinks Tournament. He has represented Memphis in the USGA Public

Links on five occasions. Thurman won the Sickle Cell Open five times and holds the tournament record of 12 under par for 36 holes.

Mr. Thurman Glass was inducted into the Memphis Amateur Golf Hall of Fame in 1993. When asked about his greatest honor in golf, he replied, "Getting to play in the Pro-Am of the Danny Thomas (Memphis Classic) a couple of times has to be number one."

Thurman Glass: a self-taught legend. Thurman Glass became interested in golf by watching the patrons of Colonial Country Club. At the age of 10, he and his neighborhood playmates began Sandlot Golf by digging holes in a vacant lot in the neighborhood. With the unwavering support of family and friends, Thurman pursued his passion for golf. In the absence of golf teams and instructors, Thurman learned the art of a golf swing by watching professionals and committing himself to endless hours of practice. Thurman Glass is one of the most celebrated amateur golfers in the greater Mid-South.

Thurman Glass has a sixty-year career of consistently winning at golf. He is humble and recognizes his gift to play golf as a God-given talent. One has to wonder, how far on the PGA Tour could Thurman Glass have climbed had not racism predetermined him "Out of Bounds."

## ANNOUNCING THE THURMAN GLASS SCHOLARSHIP

Thurman Glass, Jr., a native Memphian, began his love for golf at the tender age of 10 as he watched adults play at Colonial Country Club. Soon after, he and some friends began 'sandlot' golfing by digging holes in a neighborhood field. Surrounded by family and friends, Thurman pursued his interest in golf. Despite never receiving lessons or being part of an organized team during his school years, Thurman mastered the art of golf by watching other players and practicing for endless hours.

Thurman has received numerous awards and achievements, been featured in many newspaper articles, and won over 75 golf tournaments during his illustrious career. His first tournament win was the Sam Quarles Tournament in 1962. Thurman was a three-time winner of The Ted Rhodes Tournament (the Super Bowl of golf tournaments for African American golfers), the Memphis Publinks Tournament (which features the best local golfers and was his first integrated tournament), and the Memphis Senior Publinks Tournament. Thurman has been honored with the following accolades: a Legends of Golf Honoree (2004), induction into The Memphis Golf Hall of Fame, the Scholarship Golf Tournament First Flight (2022), and the Scholarship Golf Tournament Longest Drive (2022). He has traveled throughout the country pursuing his passion.

With a very humble spirit, Thurman believes people give him too much credit for his golfing ability and attributes the longevity of his distinguished career to being blessed beyond measure with a natural God-given gift and loving to do what God has given him.

*Dr. L. LaSimba M. Gray, Jr.*

# LONNIE "DOLLAR" SANDERS
# (1899-1992)

Lonnie "Dollar" Sanders was born in Memphis, Tennessee in 1899. At the tender age of eight, he was introduced to golf at the Memphis Country Club as a caddie. He fell in love with the game and enjoyed being around the Country Club setting. He was well-mannered and became a favorite both in and out of the caddie shack. Lonnie received many favors from the patrons of the Memphis Country Club, often receiving golf clubs, balls, and gloves. He earned his nickname because he always had a dollar in his pocket for lunch.

He studied and mastered the game of golf and excelled in caddie competitions. In 1953, he saved enough money to go to Sears and Roebuck and purchase his complete set of golf clubs and bag for $24. In 1946, Dollar Sanders won his first golf tournament in Chicago. He was then on the road with his partner, "Bubba Jeter," chasing the little white ball and green dollars on the "Chitlin Circuit" of golf for African Americans.

The dynamic duo from Memphis became known and respected on the United Golf Association Tour. The challenge was to beat the best competition and win a little extra change. The tour of the United Golf Association always made provisions for both professional and amateur golfers. In the amateur division, Dollar would sponsor Pleas Jones to expose him to national competition.

Dollar Sanders, standing 5'6" and weighing a total of 160 pounds, stood with the best on and off the golf course. He developed a reputation as a winner and gentleman. The ongoing competition between Bubba Jeter and Dollar Sanders made them better golfers and prepared them for the golfing circuit. They were prime examples of the proverbial saying, "iron sharpens iron."

When tournaments were announced, participants right away wanted to know if Dollar and Bubba were playing. Tournament directors would send out publicity, making it known when Dollar and Bubba had signed up to play.

Lonnie Sanders won the Central State Golf Tournament out of St. Louis a total of seven times, the International Senior Championship in Puerto Rico in 1963, and the National Negro Senior Championship sponsored by the United Golf Association in 1953. After winning 111 trophies, he took on a new challenge: to shoot his age. He took great delight in shooting his age beginning in his 70s.

In addition to golf, Lonnie Sanders was the owner and part owner of two businesses that allowed him to travel and spend time on the golf course. He operated the "Silver Dollar" Bar and Grill on Airways in Orange Mound and a cleaning business.

The spiritual side of Lonnie "Dollar" Sanders is well known by family and close friends, but few in the public know of his tenure at the Howe Institute in Memphis. The Howe Institute is a famous, well-respected school for preachers. Alumni and students include the legendary Rev. C.L. Franklin, father of Aretha Franklin, Bishop J.O. Patterson, Sr., Rev. Jasper Williams, Sr., Mordecai Johnson, and W.E.B. DuBois.

Lonnie "Dollar" Sanders credits his longevity and agility to "clean living and the blessings of God." Lonnie Sanders made the transition from earth to glory in 1992.

"He was the 'Dollar' that was never devalued," wrote Bobby Hall, the iconic sportswriter for *The Commercial Appeal*, on July 1, 1974.

*Dr. L. LaSimba M. Gray, Jr.*

## "THE ADDED INCENTIVE"

At the age of 76, Dollar Sanders reported, "I win money every time I play. Without the hustle, what would golf be?"

Golf had a magnetic pull on gamblers from day one. Caddies who mastered winning at any cost became known as "golfing hustlers." This group traveled from city to city looking for a game. Often their handicaps were unknown and were not publicized.

The unknown could lead to defeat and the loss of bets. Deception was utilized quite a bit. The man to beat at certain courses was often in heated competition, a golfer would read his opponent's bag to see what club was being used. In a casual manner, he would move closer to the bag and observe.

In the case of "Bubba" Jeter, one could be deceived into using too much club or not enough club. Memphis was well-known as the place to get a game but according to Pleas Jones, "Nashville was the gambling capital. You could get bets from $4.00 to $4,000."

Another dimension of the hustle was betting on "my man." A golfer did not have to bet on himself. Members of the gallery would bet on golfers. Golfers would travel in groups to gamble – gambling was the added incentive to golf. From the fairway to putting greens, bets of all sizes were made during a day on the course.

Pete Brown, commenting on the hustlers at the Fox Hills Golf Course in Los Angeles, said, "they'd be waiting, like buzzards." The buzzard waits and watches for its prey, just as the hustlers of golf courses did. The innocent, naïve, and uninformed often became prey for the hustlers.

Friendly bets include "Skins," Two-Man Scramble," "Nassau," "Rabbits," and Stroke play vs Match play. Even more friendly were bets for a coke, beer, or hot dog.

*In betting while playing golf, always remember, "Luck is overrated" – Professional Gambler.*

## Out Of Bounds: The History of African Americans and Golf in Memphis

*Had it not been for an obviously successful career in boxing, legendary boxing champion Joe Louis might have enjoyed a successful career in golf. Louis enjoyed golfing in Memphis — and Memphis golfers enjoy collecting on friendly wagers on the links.*

When African American touring professional golfers came to Memphis for St. Jude or the PGA Tour Tournaments, they made their way to Douglas and T.O. Fuller Golf Courses. They knew they could get a game in Memphis.

In search of a game, Joe "The Brown Bomber" Louis would come to Memphis! His host was Dr. H.H. Johnson, the doctor of Beale Street. The home of Dr. Johnson, on South Parkway, provided creative comforts and privacy. Joe Louis was known for his big bets and deep pockets.

> *"Golf can best be defined as an endless series of tragedies obscured by the occasional miracle"* – unknown.

From the very beginning of golf, wagering was its sidekick. Brent Kelly, award-winning sports journalist, wrote, "Golf and gambling go hand in glove for many golfers."

The motive for gambling in golf on the African American circuit included ego and bragging rights. Then there were a few who made extra money for Christmas and vacations on the golf course.

Gambling has four elements: consideration of your skills, the skills of your opponent, the risk, and the reward.

Pleas Jones, speaking of the Chitlin Circuit of African American Golfers, stated, "Nashville was the gambling capital of Black Golf. You could get bets from four dollars to four thousand dollars." It was no secret there were touring African Americans who traveled all over the country, chasing the little white ball and the green dollar.

They traveled without published handicaps. There were major tactics in winning. There were none better than Robert "Bubba" Jeter at finding a path to victory.

Andrew "Joe Bear" Bryant said, "Bubba Jeter could break down a five iron and hit it like a nine iron. He then could dial up an eight iron and hit it like a five iron." Robert "Bubba" Jeter had learned this skill out of necessity and limited access to golf clubs. When he first learned the game of golf, he had to use what he had.

From the driving range to the putting green, bets were made. Bets came in many forms and sizes; one could play for a Coke and sandwich or green fee. On a more serious note, golfers would come to T.O. Fuller and Pine Hill and bet a week's salary.

## Out Of Bounds: The History of African Americans and Golf in Memphis

Then there were professional "hustlers" who made their living on the United Golfers Association Tour. In the era of segregation, there was a real challenge to get from Memphis to Chicago or St. Louis, Detroit, Cleveland, and other major stops on the tour.

These challenges were the barriers put up by the Jim Crow Era. When the travel guide was first published, there were thousands of towns labeled "sundown towns," meaning it was high risk to travel through such towns after dark. To navigate the limited places to purchase gas, lodging, and restaurants, there was the Negro Motorist Green Book published by Victor Hugo Green out of New York, New York.

This was a travel guide to restaurants, motels, private homes, and gas stations that would serve African Americans on the road. The traveling theme was "Carry your Green Book with you; you may need it." The last edition was published in 1964. Two factors that ended the necessity of the Negro Motorist Green Book were the opening of the US Interstate Highway System and the passage of the 1964 Civil Rights Bill.

The professional golfers of the UGA had to travel and learn the tricks of the trade visiting cities where African Americans could play a course and get a game. In order to get a game, it was best to know who was "the man" to beat.

In Nashville, the man to beat was Ted Rhodes. In Los Angeles, they were Lee Elder and Bill Spiller. In Detroit, the man to beat was Joe Louis.

In Charlotte, North Carolina, the man was Charlie Sifford. In the Jackson, Mississippi area, the man to beat was Pete Brown. In Jackson, Tennessee, Rex Curry and Will Shaw were the men to beat.

When it came to Memphis, there were several men to beat: Lonnie "Dollar" Sanders, Robert "Bubba" Jeter, Mason West, Elton Grandberry, Pleas Jones, Thurman Glass, Don Holmes, and Walter Anderson. From week to week, African Americans and Caucasian golfers made their way to Memphis to play the best in Memphis.

*Dr. L. LaSimba M. Gray, Jr.*

*Above: Segregation forced African Americans to make other accommodations when they traveled -- including golfers. Dr. H. H. Johnson routinely hosted celebrities at his Memphis home on South Parkway. Heavyweight Boxing Champ Joe Louis stayed here on golf trips.*

Joe Louis, Heavyweight Boxing Champion of the World, made many trips to Memphis. He was hosted by Dr. H.H. Johnson in his home on South Parkway East. Even Joe Louis couldn't stay at the Peabody. He played at Douglas Golf Course and T.O. Fuller Golf Course. Joe Louis was a good golfer who made big bets and had deep pockets. In Memphis, the Champ had to dig deeply into his pockets on a frequent basis.

## ROBERT "BUBBA" JETER

Robert "Bubba" Jeter was born in Lee County, Arkansas, in 1908. His family relocated to Memphis while he was in grade school. In Memphis, he had the good fortune to meet and become friends with Lonnie "Dollar" Sanders.

Dollar Sanders introduced Bubba Jeter to golf at the Memphis Country Club. Initially, Bubba's interest was only to make some money. Little did he know that he was launching a life-long friendship with Dollar Sanders and a journey in the world of golf on the United Golf Association Tour.

In the 1930s, he helped organize the Eureka Golf Club. This club approached the Memphis Park Commission in 1939 about building a top-quality golf course for African Americans in Memphis. The name was later changed to honor one of the founders, Sam Qualls.

The club work was carried on by Sam Qualls, Jr., Robert "Bubba" Jeter, Rob Wright, Dr. H.H. Johnson, and Lonnie "Dollar" Sanders. The mission of the Eureka Golf Club led to the development of the Douglas Golf Course in the Douglas Community. The construction began in 1945, and the grand opening was celebrated in 1951.

Robert "Bubba" Jeter joined Dollar Sanders in teaching golf at the newly opened facility under the management of Rob Wright, the club professional.

Robert "Bubba" Jeter became a student of golf when money was hard to come by, and golf clubs were expensive. He learned to "make do" with what he had, and the few clubs given to him by white golfers.

On the United Golf Association Tour and locally, he became known as the "magician with a golf club in hand." In the words of Andrew "Bear" Bryant, "Bubba Jeter could break down a five iron and hit it like a nine iron, and then he could dial up a seven iron and hit it like a five iron." No competitor could base his club selection on what club Bubba Jeter used on any given shot.

Robert "Bubba" Jeter was a constant winner on the United Golf Association Tour and was the man to beat in local competition. He enjoyed great success as a senior but was limited by age and chronic illnesses. In his prime, he won the Central State Championship.

Charles Hudson, retired Club Professional at Pine Hill Golf, playing a round with his father and Bubba Jeter, witnessed Bubba Jeter shoot a 27 on the front nine at T.O. Fuller Golf Course. "It was unbelievable, and unfortunately, Bubba Jeter became ill and could not finish the back nine."

Mason West holds the documented record of the T.O. Fuller Course, an eight-under-par 63, in 1966. One has to wonder what the course record would have been if Robert "Bubba" Jeter had been able to finish the back nine the day he shot 27 on the front nine. It makes one wonder.

Robert "Bubba" Jeter made his transition in 1984. Rest in Peace, our hero and legend.

## PLEAS JONES, JR.:
## A GENTELMAN WHO PLAYED GOLF

From the tender age of ten, Pleas Jones Jr. was swinging clubs and chasing dreams on the greens of the Frederick Douglass Golf Course in North Memphis. Under the watchful eye of Lonnie "Dollar" Sanders, whom he served as a caddie, Pleas absorbed more than just the game; he learned life's finer values like honesty, fairness, and respect—qualities he carried throughout his career.

With Sanders, Pleas traveled the storied "Chitlin Circuit" of the United Golf Association, learning the ropes and realities of golf amid the shadows of segregation. His role as a caddie evolved as he witnessed and opposed racial barriers firsthand, particularly under the mentorship of trailblazers like Teddy Rhodes and Charlie Sifford at local tournaments.

Pleas's resolve was tested and strengthened in these early days. When the City of Memphis desegregated golf courses in 1963, he was among the first African Americans to tee off at the Audubon Golf Course—a moment marred by bigotry when a white man kicked his golf cart. Yet, Pleas never swayed; he let his prowess with the clubs do the talking. By 1961, he had already clinched the first of five consecutive titles at the Sam Qualls Golf Tournament.

His battle against segregation took a strategic turn when he teamed up with Robert Elliott, a formidable advocate for desegregation. Together, they challenged the exclusionary practices of rural West Tennessee country clubs, a campaign enriched by federal lawsuits and quiet victories on the greens. Their partnership, which lasted until Elliott's death in 2010, left an indelible mark on the sport and the community, integrating clubs that had long upheld discriminatory policies.

*Dr. L. LaSimba M. Gray, Jr.*

*Sir Pleas Jones, Jr.*

*Out Of Bounds: The History of African Americans and Golf in Memphis*

*Pleas Jones, Jr. receiving the championship in a citywide golf tournament.*

Throughout his illustrious career, Pleas won not only tournaments but hearts and respect, earning his place as a gentleman of the game. His impact extended beyond the fairways; he mentored young golfers, served on the Golf Advisory Board of the Memphis Park Commission, and ensured that the proceeds from the Pleas Jones Open benefitted local schools.

His legacy was cemented when he was inducted into the Memphis Park Commission Golf Hall of Fame on December 6, 1993—a testament to a life well-played and barriers well-broken. Pleas Jones Jr. was not just a player of golf; he was a player for change, embodying the spirit of resilience and grace on and off the golf course.

*Dr. L. LaSimba M. Gray, Jr.*

## CHARLES HUDSON

Following the long drought between Rob Wright at Douglas Golf Course and Johnny Scott at T.O. Fuller, Charles Hudson was appointed the head pro at Pine Hill Golf Course on January 1, 1989.

On January 1, 1962, Cleophus Hudson, Sr., Charles Hudson's father, was the first African American to play at Pine Hill, which was the city of Memphis' first desegregated golf course.

Prior to this historic appointment, Hudson had spent eighteen years with the Memphis chapter of the Boys Club.

The immediate difference Hudson made at Pine Hill was his focus on youth. He recognized the transformative power of mentorship and supervision in outdoor activities.

He organized the Mid-South Junior Golf Program with the clear goal of introducing African American youth to golf, but Hudson's mission went deeper: it was about youth development.

Charles gathered a group of interested golfers and a few trusted friends, wrote the constitution and bylaws, and applied for 501(c)(3) status from the Internal Revenue Service. Charlie Wilson, Calvin Vinson, and Melba Vinson joined the movement.

The concept of a golfing program that extended beyond mere introduction to golf was enthusiastically embraced by corporate Memphis. Support was offered by Federal Express, International Paper, and Schering Plough.

Calvin Vinson took on the role of president and emphatically made it clear to the parents of potential participants what to expect. A special emphasis was placed on punctuality and respect.

"If you are working for the next Tiger Woods, this is not the program for your child," he said. "We are promoting youth development."

The program received a real boost when local PGA golfer Lauren Roberts joined the instructional staff. He volunteered to teach the basics of golf, along with swing and putting techniques.

The program expanded rapidly. In 1992, the volunteers prepared for the annual clinic, expecting 20 to 30 participants, and were met with an enrollment of 88. Young people registered from areas ranging from Germantown to Boxtown, from South Memphis to East Memphis.

The program, an idea whose time had come, made its presence felt at Pine Hill Course. Charles Hudson's dedication was highlighted in 1997 when Tiger Woods came to support the Mid-South Junior Golf program on the day of the clinic and exhibition.

There was not a hotter ticket in town than what Charles Hudson achieved with the Mid-South Junior Golf program, which parallels what Tiger Woods is accomplishing with his foundation. Tiger did not visit the Colonial Country Club, nor the Southwest Country Club; he came to Pine Hill Golf Course in South Memphis.

Hudson has been celebrated and recognized for his work, but the greatest compliment was paid when Lauren Roberts said of Charles Hudson, "No one in Memphis has done more for golf."

*Dr. L. LaSimba M. Gray, Jr.*

## REX CURRY

Professor Rex Curry, Sr. is pictured receiving the trophy at the first Annual Lane Alumni Golf Tournament in Jackson, Tennessee, in 1970 at the McKellar Golf Course.

The Lane Alumni Golf Tournament was the first golf tournament I organized. I was advised by the head pro of McKellar to use the Callaway Handicapping system for a one-day golf tournament. The issue was fairness and the best way to establish a one-day handicap, as the golfers had come from all over the country, and no one had an established handicap. This was a fun weekend of reunions, dances, alumni meetings, and the newly added Alumni golf tournament.

The Callaway System only allowed a "double bogey" on a given hole and then allowed the golfer to deduct the worst score. The net score is then calculated, determining the winner. In the first Lane Alumni golf tournament, the Alumni and Head Basketball coach at Lane was the medalist. When the Callaway handicapping index was applied, Professor Rex Curry, principal of East High, won the tournament. Willie Shaw, who was a great sport, would annually remind me, "Gray, don't ever use that Callaway System again."

# JASPER PHILLIPS
# (1903 - 1991)

Jasper Phillips was my uncle.

He was born in Pleasant Hill, Mississippi, in 1903 and made his way to Shelby County, Tennessee, in the early 1900s. He attended Capleville School and developed a love for the outdoors on the family farm. He raised and trained dogs for hunting rabbits.

Alongside his siblings, he helped his parents, Edgar Phillips and Armentha, manage the arduous system of sharecropping. At the tender age of 25, he left the farm for the big city of Memphis. There, he found work at the Cherokee Country Club as a greenskeeper.

When the site had to move due to the construction of the new interstate highway in the early 1960s, Jasper was invited by Earl Dykema to relocate and continue his work as a greenskeeper at the new Windyke Country Club.

In the spring of 1985, Jasper retired and departed this life on Monday, July 29, 1991.

*Dr. L. LaSimba M. Gray, Jr.*

## JIMMIE "PECKER" FIELDS
### A PINE HILL LEGEND

Jimmie "Pecker" Fields was born in Hickory Whithe, Tennessee, now present-day Arlington, Tennessee. As a teenager, he found his way to Memphis, where he secured a job and enrolled at Booker T. Washington High School. Later, he attended LeMoyne College and was drafted by Uncle Sam to serve in the Korean conflict.

With an honorable discharge, "Pecker" returned to Memphis, where he met and married his wife, Mable. He took up golf and became a regular at Pine Hill and T.O. Fuller Golf Courses. He earned the nickname "Pecker" because of his short but consistent drives and iron shots—always in the middle. This was referred to as 'pecking the ball'.

In 2005, Charles Hudson, Club Pro at Pine Hill, joined OTG Golfers to name a monument in honor of Jimmie Fields. "Pecker's Ridge," located on the 9th hole, reminds all golfers that "Pecker" had been there.

According to "Pecker," he held the record for the most holes-in-one golf shots. He proudly claimed, and was never disputed, to have made six holes-in-one at Pine Hill Golf Course. Jimmie Jackson "Pecker" Fields is truly a legend at Pine Hill Golf Course. Rest in Peace.

---

**"AMBUSHED" BY JIMMIE "PECKER" FIELDS**

*I returned to Memphis in 1973 and played T.O. Fuller on a regular basis. I decided to play Pine Hill for a change-up. As I approached the clubhouse, this small man with a stutter approached me. "Mind if I join you?" "Sure, you can," was my response.*

*As we approached No. 1, he said, "I have to have a little bet." I thought about his size and demeanor and said, "Yes." He said, "What about a dollar a hole and two down automatic?"*

*By the time we reached No. 7, I realized I had been ambushed by the "Pecker." Jimmie Fields never allowed me to forget that encounter, and I never did.*

— LaSimba

*Out Of Bounds: The History of African Americans and Golf in Memphis*

*Jimmie "Pecker" Fields*

*Dr. L. LaSimba M. Gray, Jr.*

## CELEBRATING THE LIFE OF GENE AUSTIN FENTRESS

Gene "Geno" Fentress made golfing history.

His sterling career spanned coaching sports at Alcy Elementary School, serving as Labor Relations Manager at Blue Cross and Blue Shield of Memphis, and working in various capacities that highlighted his natural affinity for working with people.

Known as a "people person," Gene was a tremendous asset to the Urban Youth Ministries, the Workforce Redevelopment with the Private Industry Council, and First Tennessee Bank.

During the affirmative action era of Corporate Memphis, Gene Fentress was recruited by First Tennessee Bank and promoted to become the first African American Branch Manager. Upon reading the employee handbook, particularly the benefits section, he discovered that as an officer of the bank, he had playing privileges at the prestigious Memphis Country Club—the first golf club in Memphis.

A glitch, however, arose in the hiring process of Gene Fentress: his golfing abilities were never discussed.

Deciding to utilize these privileges, Gene went to the Memphis Country Club to introduce himself and play a round of golf. He was met in the parking lot and abruptly told, "Not here. A mistake has been made." Despite being within the policy provisions, Gene was not allowed to play, and the integration of the Memphis Country Club was consequently delayed.

Gene Fentress, a graduate of Tennessee State University, excelled in basketball and football and was a member of the wrestling club. At Tennessee State, he pledged Omega Psi Phi Fraternity, Inc. and proposed to the beautiful Ruby Price from Sparta, Tennessee.

After graduation, they married and had one daughter, now attorney Lorri Fentress Priestley, and one grandson, Austin "Junebug" Priestley. An avid golfer, Gene was a founding member of the Pro-Golfers South of Memphis Golf Club.

*Dr. L. LaSimba M. Gray, Jr.*

# JERRY "CAP" BUTLER
## MEMPHIS LEGEND IN AMERICAN GOLF

Jerry "Cap" Butler grew up in the Riverside community of South Memphis. He attended Carver High School and played football, basketball, and golf. He was always chosen as the leader of the various teams he played on. Coach William "Woody" Woodruff recognized his leadership, giving Jerry the nickname "Cap," which was short for captain. Coach Woodruff exposed young Jerry to the best African American golfers in the Memphis/Shelby County area.

Upon graduation in 1974, Jerry Butler was recognized as one of the best high school golfers in the State of Tennessee. He had an average score of 71.2 in the state competition.

With the support of Coach Woodruff, Jerry was awarded a golfing scholarship to Southern University in Baton Rouge, Louisiana. At Southern, Jerry competed in the Southern Western Athletic Conference (SWAC).

Jerry Butler, upon arriving in Baton Rouge, began collecting trophies and winning honors. He was a golfing force to be reckoned with. From 1974 – 1978, he won ten (10) championships in collegiate golf and was named to the All-American Golf Team for four (4) consecutive years. In 1978, he won the SWAC Individual Championship.

In 2016, Jerry "Cap" Butler was inducted into the Southern University Athletic Hall of Fame.

# SPECIAL NOTES OF AFRICAN AMERICANS AND GOLF IN MEMPHIS, TENNESSEE

**Mason West** held the documented course record at T. O. Fuller, an eight (8) under par 63, for many years. **Charles Hudson** joined his father in a foursome that included **Robert "Bubba" Jeter** one Saturday morning at T. O. Fuller and witnessed what he called "the greatest exhibition of golf I ever saw in Memphis."

On the front nine, "Bubba" Jeter shot an unbelievable score of 27." Charles Hudson went on to say, "Unfortunately, Mr. Jeter became ill on the back nine and could not finish. It is safe to say because of an illness the course record of 63 still stands."

**Donald Holmes** was a teenager in 1973 when the first Sickle Cell Anemia Open was played at T.O. Fuller Golf Course, and he came in fourth in the Championship Flight. As preparations were being made to distribute trophies, E. F. Gray, an uncle to Don Holmes, petitioned the tournament officials to recognize the young Don Holmes for his outstanding play. From the inaugural tournament to this date, no other golfer has won the championship trophy and the green jacket as many times as Donald "DH" Holmes. Donald Holmes holds the tournament record for consecutive wins of six (6) straight victories from 1987 through 1992. In the first 25 years of the Sickle Cell Open, Don Holmes won the Championship a total of eleven (11) times.

**Thurman Glass** holds the Sickle Cell Open Tournament record of twelve (12) under par in 1985. He is followed closely by Walter Anderson with eleven (11) under par in 1980. Thurman won the Sickle Cell Open in 1974, 1978, 1982, 1985, and 1986. Thurman was self-taught by observing the swing of golfers at the Colonial Country Club and then spent hours in practice to duplicate the swing.

**Pleas Jones, Jr.** won the First Sickle Cell Open Tournament in 1973 with a score of six (6) under par. In 1969, Pleas Jones won the Memphis Publinx Tournament, which featured amateur golfers of all races and creeds. He won his second Memphis Publinx Tournament in 1975 and served on the Memphis Park Commission Golf Advisory Board. He worked as an instructor in the Sam Qualls Junior Golf Clinic as a teenager.

**Lonnie "Dollar" Sanders** was introduced to golf as a caddy at the Memphis Country Club and began playing golf at Lincoln Park Golf Course, the Douglas Golf Course, and the T. O. Fuller Golf Course. He took on Pleas Jones Jr. as his caddy at the Douglas Golf Course and taught Pleas the game. "Dollar" Sanders became the most admired and respected African American golfer in the Mid-South. Standing at 5'6" and weighing 160 pounds, no African American has stood taller in the world of golf. He traveled the United Golf Association circuit for more than fifty (50) years. He was a professional baseball player with the Memphis Red Sox Team in the Negro Baseball League. He attended the legendary Howe Institute in Memphis, known to train Ministers of the gospel.

**Robert "Bubba" Jeter** was introduced to golf by Dollar Sanders at the Memphis Country Club. The first chance he got, he joined the United Golf Association Tour and became the first African American from Memphis to play golf for a living. "Bubba" Jeter played on the Pro-Circuit and continued to play the amateur circuit as a Senior Competitor. One could always find "Bubba's" name in the winner's column for most African American Golf Tournaments across the United States.

**Walter Anderson** won the Sickle Cell Open in 1976 with a seven (7) under-par score in a field of 150 players. He won his second Sickle Cell Open in 1980 with a score of eleven (11) under in a field of 164 players. Walter Anderson won the 1983 Sickle Cell Open with a score of nine (9) under in a field of 197 players.

*Introduced to golf by his father, Greg Odom Jr. is a rising star on the PGA Tour.*

# THE NEW HORIZON

This historical preservation of African American Golfers in Memphis is critical to paving the way for the next generation.

The next generation will include the likes of Will Keys, Managing Professional at Pine Hills; Greg Odom, Jr., a rising star on the PGA tour from Memphis; and John Parks Thornton, who is still following his dream of playing professional golf after a stellar collegiate career at Texas Southern. Currently, Thornton is on the APGA Tour (Advocates Professional Golf Association). In the summer of 2020, Thornton won his first professional victory in the APGA at the TPC Sugarloaf.

Greg Odom was introduced to golf by his father, Greg Odom Senior. He led the Howard University Golf Team to their first collegiate championship. Odom was then recognized as HBCU golfer of the year and named an All-American in 2022.

Stephen Curry of the Golden State Warriors has committed to funding the Howard University Golf Program for six years and personally agreed to mentor Greg Odom, Jr.

Speaking of Greg, Stephen Curry stated, "He has amazing talent to get him on the PGA Tour, to get some experience, continue to wave that (our) flag is going to be awesome."

Greg Odom, Jr. and John Parks Thornton will be a source of inspiration for generations unborn. The Memphis legends like Robert "Bubba" Jeter, Mason West, Dollar Sanders, Pleas Jones Jr., and Thurman Glass will witness a new day in Memphis Golf. PGA Tour victories by Memphians are looming, Ryder Cup teams will have a Memphis flavor, and the green jackets of the Masters will have to be tailored to fit the likes of Greg Odom, Jr. and John Parks Thornton.

It is a new day in Memphis Golf. Racial barriers have been removed from public view. When we learn about the challenges that prevented the legends from the gateway to professional golf, we can and must direct our energy to eliminate those challenges.

The new generation of rising stars will have options that Ted Rhodes, Bill Spiller, Charlie Sifford, and Lee Elder never had: the LIV Professional Golf Tour. The LIV was created in 2021 by the Public Investment Fund, the Sovereign Wealth Fund of Saudi Arabia.

Greg Norman serves as CEO. The inaugural season was in 2021. This tour has many differences, but the main difference is it does not have a "Caucasian only clause" in its constitution. Secondly, the tour has wells of money.

The LIV tour only plays 54 holes, which is a real advantage for aging players. Golfers only play three rounds with a lucrative payout system.

## Out Of Bounds: The History of African Americans and Golf in Memphis

Dr. L. LaSimba M. Gray, Jr.

# BEST DRESSED GOLFERS IN MEMPHIS

Not only were these golfers phenomenal players, many were also known to dress to impress on the tees. *The Commercial Appeal* once featured an article naming some of these golfers as the best dressed in Memphis.
Those who made the list of the Best Dressed included:

Pleas Jones, Jr.<br>
Eddie Lowe<br>
Walter Evans<br>
Charlie Wilson<br>
Robert Crawford<br>
Willie Lomax<br>
Thomas Lomax<br>
Odessa Dickens<br>
Carey Jones<br>
Leon Griffin

*Left: Plenty of Memphis Golfers had style to go with their games. From top left: Pleas Jones Jr., Thomas Lomax, Charlie Wilson, Willie Lomax and Charlie Wilson. Representing the ladies front and center is Carey Jones.*

*Dr. L. LaSimba M. Gray, Jr.*

*Out Of Bounds: The History of African Americans and Golf in Memphis*

# THE MEMPHIS AMATEUR GOLF HALL OF FAME

# AFRICAN AMERICAN INDUCTEES

Memphis has long been a cradle of talent in the world of golf, particularly evident in the remarkable achievements of its African American players. The Memphis Amateur Hall of Fame stands as a proud testament to these extraordinary individuals who have not only excelled in their sport but have also carved a path for others to follow.

Their inclusion in this esteemed Hall of Fame is more than an acknowledgment of their skill and victories; it represents a journey of determination, skill, and unwavering passion for the game. These individuals have transcended barriers and have become synonymous with excellence in golf, contributing immensely to Memphis's rich golfing heritage.

**Thurman Glass, Jr.**
**Odessa Dickens Hayes**
**Pleas Jones, Jr.**
**Dalton Nickleberry, Sr.**
**Polk McCray**
**Lonnie "Dollar" Sanders**
**Fred Jones***

*\*Inducted into the Amateur Sports Hall of Fame*

*Dr. L. LaSimba M. Gray, Jr.*

*Out Of Bounds: The History of African Americans and Golf in Memphis*

# LEGENDARY AFRICAN AMERICAN GOLFERS OF MEMPHIS AND THE MID-SOUTH

As we turn the pages of Memphis' storied golf history, we pause to honor the African American golf legends who have left an indelible mark on its fairways.

These individuals, celebrated for their skill, perseverance, and pioneering spirit, transcended the challenges of their times to master the game they loved. Their legacy is not just in the strokes and scores but in the barriers, they broke and the paths they paved for future generations.

This is a tribute to their enduring impact and a reminder of their contributions that forever changed the landscape of golf in Memphis.

Robert "Bubba" Jeter
Lonnie "Dollar" Sanders
Cleophus Hudson
Charlie Wilson
Walter Anderson
Mason West
Elton Grandberry
Sam Quales, Jr.
Pleas Jones
Thurman Glass
Donald Holmes
Ms. Odessa Dickens
Lillie Crockett
Jerry Butler
Randy Perry
Dalton Nickleberry, Sr.

*Dr. L. LaSimba M. Gray, Jr.*

# IN MEMORIAM: AFRICAN AMERICAN GOLF LEGENDS OF MEMPHIS

In remembrance and honor, we pay tribute to the African American golf legends of Memphis, whose skills, determination, and pioneering spirit have left an indelible mark on the fairways of history.

These legends, who navigated the complexities of both the sport and societal challenges, have carved a path of excellence, not only in Memphis but in the hearts of all who admire the game. Their legacy, a blend of talent, resilience, and unwavering dedication, has laid the foundation for future generations, turning obstacles into opportunities.

This memorial serves as a testament to their enduring impact, ensuring that their contributions to golf and their community are never forgotten.

**Lonnie "Dollar" Sanders**
**Willie Burkins**
**Charlie Wilson**
**Gene Fentress**
**Cleophus Hudson, Sr.**
**Nathaniel Miller**
**Odessa Dickens**
**Leon Griffin**
**Walter Evans**
**Wade Scott**
**Cornelius Burkins**
**Calvin Porter**
**Robert "Bubba" Jeter**
**Jimmie "The Pecker" Fields**

*Dr. L. LaSimba M. Gray, Jr.*

# IN MEMORIAM: THE COURAGEOUS MEN WHO FILED THE LAWSUIT WATSON V. CITY OF MEMPHIS

In a pivotal chapter of Memphis' golf history, a courageous group of African American golfers stood against the tides of exclusion and discrimination by filing a lawsuit against the City of Memphis.

This legal battle, more than just a fight for fair access to golf courses, was a bold stand for equality and justice in the face of systemic barriers. Their unwavering determination and legal action not only paved the way for future generations of golfers regardless of race but also marked a significant step towards the desegregation of public spaces in Memphis.

The legacy of these golfers extends beyond the fairways; it is etched in the broader narrative of civil rights and social change, embodying the spirit of resilience and the pursuit of equality.

Attorney A. W. Willis
Attorney Ben L. Hooks
Attorney Russell B. Sugarmon
Melvin Malundai
Dr. T.W. Northcross
Dr. W.O. Speight
Johnny Gholston
Harold Gholston
Alfred Haynes, Jr.
John Rogers
Thomas Pugh
Curtis King
Dr. Ike A. Watson, Jr.
Dr. Arthur E. Horne

*Dr. L. LaSimba M. Gray, Jr.*

# MEMPHIS AREA SANDLOT COURSES

## CASTALIA HEIGHTS LOCATION:

Behind the Castalia supermarket located on Castalia Street was a vacant lot. Neighborhood caddies got permission and built a whole golf course. The builders were Andrew "Joe Bear" Bryant, Vernon Townsend, Roy "Pony" Scott, Percy Dolman, Robert "Grass Hopper" Dolman, and Cleveland Rankin.

These men had contracted the "golf fever" as caddies at Cherokee and Fox Meadows Country Clubs. The Castalia Sandlot Course was only four holes, but provided unlimited pleasure for African American golfers, who were deemed out of bounds at area golf courses.

## LINCOLN PARK LOCATION:

Locations: Blakemore and Menager streets were the eastern borders. There was an exchange off Bellevue, now Elvis Presley, near the Cane Creek Baptist Church. The park was opened in 1935 with a seven-hole golf course included.

When the Lincoln Park golf course was closed in 1951, neighborhood golfers continued with the maintenance of a few of the holes that existed earlier. The Lincoln Garden Cafe on Menager Street served as the Club House and yet operated as the management site.

## DOUGLAS PARK LOCATION:

The Athletic Fields of Douglas High School were ideal for Sandlot sports. Lonnie "Dollar" Sanders was the chief architect and designer for the Douglas sandlot golf course.

Robert "Bubba" Jeter served as his assistant. When completed, there was a stream of eager students to learn and play golf. Dollar Sanders' primary purpose was to teach the younger generation the game of golf. Some of the early students included Pleas Jones, Eddie Lowe, Odessa Dickens, and Dalton Nickleberry.

## WHITE STATION AREA LOCATION:

This course was built on the present-day site of Home Depot located at 800 Truse Rd. in the Eastgate shopping center. Cornelius and Willie Burkins were joined by cousin David Alexander using swing blades and push lawnmowers to build a two-hole golf course.

It was an instant success and used by the neighborhood. Thurman Glass would watch golfers at Colonial Golf Country Club through the fence and then go to their two-hole sandlot golf course to practice hours at a time.

Cornelius and Willie Burkins emerged from the two-hole golf course to become well-respected golfers throughout the mid-south. Dave Alexander, a cousin, became a premier golf club builder and repairman. He worked with Willie and Cornelius at Bert Dargie and then later joined the staff at the Pickett Golf Company. Dave closed out his career running his own golf club repair shop in southeast Memphis on Getwell.

*Dr. L. LaSimba M. Gray, Jr.*

*Out Of Bounds: The History of African Americans and Golf in Memphis*

# THE PRESERVATION OF HISTORY AT PINE HILL GOLF COURSE

# PROPOSAL
# PINE HILL GOLF COURSE
# MEMPHIS, TENNESSEE

*This proposal was submitted to the City of Memphis, to preserve the history of the Pine Hill Golf Course.*

**NAME CHANGE:** From Links at Pine Hill to The Legends at Pine Hill

**RATIONALE:** To recognize and honor the many African American Golfers who defied racism and waited out racial discrimination to play the game of golf. Many learned the game while serving as caddies for the rich and famous and the "Memphis Power Structure." Segregation was stringently enforced, and "Negros" were not allowed to enter the public parks until 1963. When the United States Supreme Court ordered the desegregation of all public facilities in Memphis.

Even though African Americans made up 49% of the population in 1900, segregation excluded "Negros" from parks and other recreational outlets. Out of pure frustration and disgust, Robert R. Church, Sr. purchased a six-acre lot on Beale Street and developed the first park for African Americans. Church, a millionaire, invested $100,000 dollars in a magnificent enterprise for recreation and racial redemption. From the 1899 creation of Church Park to the ruling of the Supreme Court to end the exclusion of Negroes Sixty-three (63) golfing seasons passed into oblivion.

*A panoramic view of the scenic fairway at Pine Hills Golf Course.*

In the interim, African Americans golfers honed their skills on makeshift golf courses at the less than adequate courses at Douglas and Lincoln Parks. A few of the private country clubs allow caddies to play on designated days during the year: This practice was known as Caddy Day.

Public pressure increased on the conservative political leadership of Memphis to provide Parks and Recreational outlets. This "political football" was kicked down the proverbial road until 1913 when the City of Memphis purchased a 53-acre tract in the iconic Douglas Community in Northeast Memphis. The Douglas Parks and Golf Course were developed exclusively for African Americans to justify segregation of publicly owned facilities. A relationship between Memphis and the State of Tennessee led to the development of the Bluff State Park in 1938. The Bluff State Park was a major attraction and addition to the limited public parks for African Americans in Memphis (at State expense).

The golf courses quickly became the premier attraction for African American golfers and Tournaments, in the Mid-South. The Park was renamed in 1942 to honor Dr. T.O. Fuller, local educator, and theologian.

Unfortunately, the golf course was closed in 2011 and converted to a hiking trail.

On January 1, 1963, Cleophus Hudson lead his group consisting of Richard Powell, Lawrence Daughterly, and the First Tee at Pine Hill. Pine Hill was the first public golf course to relinquish its "Whites only" signs.

## PROPOSAL FOR THE GRAND REOPENING OF PINEHILL GOLF COURSE

**Name Change:** Legends at Pine Hill

**Rationale:** To recognize and honor the legendary amateur golfers of Memphis and the Mid-South who endured segregation and yet rose to prominence in golf.

Each of the 18 holes will have a historical marker honoring one of the legends. (See Rendering attached).

The Club House is to be named in honor of Charles Hudson, Former Professional and Founding instructor of Mid-South Junior Golf Association.

**Rationale:** Charles Hudson was taught the game of golf at the segregated Douglas Park. Golf Course by his father, Mr. Cleophus Hudson, Sr. Charles was awarded a gold scholarship at Southern University in

*Thurman Glass, Pleas Jones, Jr., and Dr. Gray were on hand for the opening of the renovated Pine Hill Golf Course.*

1962. Charles Hudson returned to Memphis and began to teach inner-city youth the game of golf.

Charles Hudson's success and faithfulness in the arena of discipline and scholarship are well-documented. He served as the resident professional for years at Pine Hill.

The proposed Hall of Fame will be housed in the new clubhouse displaying records and golfing achievements. Winners, regardless of race, of the Pine Hill Open and Memphis Publinx will be displayed in the Club House.

## PROPOSED HONORARY HOLES AT "LEGENDS AT PINE HILLS"

### CLEOPHUS HUDSON

437 Yards – Par 4
The first African American to tee off at the newly integrated Pine Hill Golf Course, Jan. 1, 1962.

### ROBERT "BUBBA" JETER

410 Yards - Par 4
Caddie, Self-Taught, Scratch Player

### LONNIE "DOLLAR" SANDERS

160 Yards – Par 3

*Dr. L. LaSimba M. Gray, Jr.*

# THE GATHERING

The "Gathering" was the beginning of Project Preservation. On May 27, 2024. African American Golfers gathered at the iconic Stein's Restaurant on South Lauderdale to eat fish and talk golf. Golfers brought photos, souvenirs, and art, along with facts to cover the story of African Americans in Memphis golf. This book, "Out of Bounds," is the byproduct of that initial meeting.

Top: Dr. Gray and Greater Memphis Chamber Charman, Willie Gregory; Middle: Bishop David Allen Hall addresses the group; Bottom: Dr. Gray and Bishop Hall.

## Out Of Bounds: The History of African Americans and Golf in Memphis

Dr. L. LaSimba M. Gray, Jr.

# AFTERTHOUGHTS OF THE AUTHOR

The focus of my afterthoughts rest upon the men who joined Dr. Ike A. Watson, Jr. in his 1960 Federal Lawsuit to end segregation in Memphis Public Golf Courses.

This courageous move required a tremendous resolve: Come hell or high water when Dr. Ike A. Watson, Jr., filed the lawsuit in 1960. He was supported by Dr. Arthur E. Horne, Dr. T.W. Northcross, Dr. W.O. Speight, Jr., Melvin Malyndai, Johnny Gholston, Harold Alfred Haynes, Jr., John Rogers, Thomas Pugh, and Curtis King.

Upon deep reflection, I pondered why these men took such a stand. I found answers in the words of Dr. George R. Kirsch, a history professor at Manhattan College, New York. 'Golf was an early battleground of the Civil Rights Movement in the United States along with Voting Rights and equal access to hotels and restaurants, transportation, playgrounds, beaches, and other public accommodations.'

The emergence of Tiger Woods from the historical and horrific treatment of African American Golfers in the 20th Century is nothing short of a miracle. When Eldrick 'Tiger' Woods was born on December 30, 1975, he was considered out of bounds by the world of golf. Tiger was completely unaware of the 'Caucasian only' clause of the Professional Golf Association's by-laws.

He was introduced to golf by his father, Earl Woods, and at the tender age of two, he made his first national television appearance, putting a golf ball. With marine toughness, Tiger was taught to control himself in the game of golf and life. Earl Woods never taught Tiger how to lose.

When the barriers of segregation and racism are considered, one must wonder what if these barriers never existed? Without the 'Caucasian only clause' of the PGA, where would the likes of Ted Rhodes, Bill Spiller, Charlie Sifford, Lee Elder, Pete Brown, and Charles Owens stand in national rankings of professional golfers?

Closer to home, where would the likes of Lonnie 'Dollar' Sanders, Robert 'Bubba' Jeter, Charlie 'Sweet Pie' Wilson, Pleas Jones, Thurman Glass, Walter Anderson, Mason West, and Elton Grandberry stand in the ranks of professional golf?

For every miracle in the Bible wrought by Jesus, human participation was a requirement. When Jesus fed the 5,000, he used the lunch of a small boy. When he turned water into wine, the disciples had to fill the water pots.

In Memphis to end segregation, human participation included Dr. Ike A. Watson, Jr., Benjamin L. Hooks, A.W. Willis, H. T. Lockhart, Russell Sugarmon, and Thurgood Marshall. Dr. Watson filed a Federal Lawsuit in 1960. Cleophus Hudson, Sr. was the first African American to tee off at Pine Hill Golf during the City of Memphis's gradual plan of desegregation.

This historic tee-off took place on January 1, 1962, at Pine Hill Golf Course. The United States Supreme Court ruled in 1963 to end segregation on Memphis Golf Courses. Pleas Jones led a group to the Audubon Golf Course to enjoy a day of golf on the historic new beginning for Memphis Golf. In his group were Odessa Dickens, Dalton Nickleberry, Sr., and Wade Scott.

It is very interesting that when the United Golf Association (UGA) was formed in 1925, it was formed to provide an alternative to the Professional Golf Association for African American Golfers. In a real sense, the United Golf Association was very much like the National Negro Baseball League.

Established out of necessity. Joe Louis, the legendary Heavyweight Boxing Champion of the world, said this of the United Golf Association: 'Well, like they say, if they won't let you join their party, have a party of your own.'

The UGA is still active and yet embraces its original mission of 1925. The same mission, after nearly 100 years, speaks volumes to the lack of progress made in changing the culture of golf. The changing of the culture begins with each African American interested in positive change in the world of golf. Questions must be pondered, and actions must take place.

One of the driving principles taught to Tiger Woods by Earl Woods is "start something." To make life better, he continues, "start dreaming, start exploring, start growing, start asking, start thinking, start going, start sailing, start imagining, start rehearsing, start picturing, start grooving, start painting, start something."

Let me suggest that we find young golfing talent in the African American Community and form financial support groups to help cover basic expenses required to become a touring professional. It has been done before and the expert is yet in our midst.

Charles Hudson was part of the African American Golf Professionals who 'passed the hat' to help Tiger Woods get started. We don't have to look far to find talent worthy of our support. John Parks Thornton and Greg Odom, Jr. are on the tee now.

Let us be that 'human participation' needed to bring about the next miracle in Memphis Golf. I am convinced that if we start something in this arena, there are individuals of goodwill of other ethnic persuasions who will help.

# ABOUT THE AUTHOR

**Dr. L. LaSimba M. Gray, Jr**. is a historical and pastoral/church consultant, author, and civil rights activist. After graduating from Lane College with a Bachelor of Science degree in 1968, he taught in St. Louis, Missouri Public Schools. In the summer of 1969, he joined the staff at Lane College in Alumni Affairs and Public Relations.

In 1973, he was hired to work at the Medical School of the University of Tennessee as the Community Coordinator for the Comprehensive Sickle Cell Anemia Program. In 1974, he received a master's degree in Education from then "Memphis State University."

That same year, he accepted his calling to ministry at the New Hope Baptist Church in Jago, Mississippi. In 1975, he enrolled at Memphis Theological Seminary, spending the next twenty years earning both a Master of Divinity and a Doctorate of Ministry degrees.

During his 40-plus years in ministry as a minister of the gospel, he served as Pastor at St. Mark Baptist Church in Atoka, Tennessee, and finally at the New Sardis Baptist Church in Memphis, Tennessee.

Dr. Gray accepted the call for the leadership of the Memphis Affiliate of the Rainbow Push Coalition in 1975 and served as an alternate delegate to the historic 1984 Democratic National Convention in San Francisco, CA, where Rev. Jesse Louis Jackson delivered one of the keynote addresses.

In 1990, Dr. Gray organized a group of activists and filed a federal lawsuit challenging the runoff provision of city elections in Memphis, alleging a violation of the 1965 Voting Rights Act. The federal court ruled, without a trial, that the runoff was unconstitutional, leading to the election of Dr. W. W. Herenton as the first African American Mayor of Memphis.

## Dr. L. LaSimba M. Gray, Jr.

He served as the Health Coordinator for the Memphis Affiliate of the Congress of National Black Churches, President of the Memphis satellite of Operation Push, and served on the Tennessee Human Rights Commission under three governors.

He taught in the Congress of the National Baptist Convention, USA, Inc., and Bluff City Christian College, in Memphis. He also served on the faculty of the Congress of Christian Education for the Baptist Association in Germany, spending 10 days in Germany, Switzerland, and Italy, teaching, touring, and preaching the Gospel of Jesus Christ. In 2010, he served on the board of licensure for social workers in the State of Tennessee.

He served as an adjunct professor for Memphis Theological Seminary and on the Board of Directors of the former Tri-State Bank of Memphis for 17 years, chairing the Development Committee. He is a proud part-owner and treasurer of the *Tri-State Defender* Newspaper and a stockholder in the "Family Tradition" 1340 WLOK Radio.

Since 2020, Dr. Gray has served as the chairman of the Memphis Memorial Committee, working to preserve the legacy and honor Ida B. Wells. The committee erected a statue in her honor in 2021 and continues to honor her through various projects, including advocating for renaming Fourth Street after her and renovating a plaza in her honor.

Dr. Gray was nurtured in the Christian faith by loving, devoted Christian parents, Reverend Leo M. Gray, Sr., and Mrs. Corine Olivia Gray. He was baptized at the Middle Baptist Church. Under the leadership of Dr. E. W. Williamson and Dr. Benjamin Lawson Hooks of the Greater Middle Baptist Church in Memphis, Dr. L. LaSimba M. Gray, Jr. was introduced to prophetic Ministry. He followed their examples of speaking "Truth to Power" and fighting injustices.

On December 5, 1999, the Shelby County Commission renamed a major section of Holmes Road in Memphis "The Dr. L. LaSimba Gray, Jr. Road" to honor Dr. Gray for his long tenure of service in Shelby County.

In February 2000, Dr. Gray made available to the general public his published book: 'Deacons for Defense and Justice.' This spellbinding book is about African American men in Bogalusa, Louisiana who armed themselves to defend their community against the KKK during the civil rights movement.

In 2020, Dr. Gray published 'Metamorphosis of Memphis: The Blues and Beale Street: 1819-2019.'

Dr. Gray enjoys relaxing, golfing, gardening, traveling, and spending time with his family. He has two daughters, Angelique Gray and Dr. Leah Gray. He takes great pride in collecting and restoring classic automobiles.

He was introduced to golf in 1963 by Albert Flowers, who used to caddy at Windyke Country Club. The late Walter Evans of Josten Jewelers gave the author his first complete set of golf clubs in 1970.

He organized his first golf tournament in 1969, the Lane College Alumni Golf Tournament in Jackson, Tennessee, at the McKellar Golf Course. In 1973, he was hired by the University of Tennessee School of Medicine to coordinate the Memphis Regional Sickle Cell America Comprehensive Outreach.

In 1973, he founded the Sickle Cell Golf Tournament in Memphis to raise awareness of the dreadful disease. The Sickle Cell Golf Tournament grew to become the largest amateur golf tournament in the Mid-South in support of Sickle Cell Anemia, attracting African American golfers from cities such as Little Rock, Dallas, Los Angeles, Chicago, Atlanta, and Jackson, Mississippi.

He holds membership at the Wyndyke Country Club, in honor of his dear friend Albert 'Spooky' Flowers. It was at Wyndyke Country Club where Albert taught him the game of golf.

# BIBLIOGRAPHY

## BIBLIOGRAPHY

- The Commercial Appeal, December 9, 1926.
- The Commercial Appeal, March 7, 1975.
- The Memphis Press-Scimitar, May 31, 1963.
- The Memphis Press-Scimitar, June 12, 1963.
- The Commercial Appeal, July 9, 1998.
- The Memphis Press-Scimitar, June 19, 1962.
- The Memphis Press-Scimitar, May 27, 1963.
- The Commercial Appeal, August 21, 1958.
- The Commercial Appeal, August 29, 1958.
- The Commercial Appeal, September 6, 1965.
- The Commercial Appeal, July 1, 1973.
- The Memphis Press-Scimitar, [Date of dedication of T.O. Fuller Park].
- The Commercial Appeal, June 17, 1968.
- The Commercial Appeal, April 17, 1963.
- Tri-State Defender, September 1956.
- Memphis World, May 1959.
- Willis Decosta, Black Landmarks, Memphis, 2010.
- Jones, Pleas. "Memphis Hall of Fame Golfer," Memphis, TN. Interviewed by L. LaSimba M. Gray, Jr., December 15, 2022.
- Burkins, Cornelieus. "Legend in Memphis Golf Culture." Interviewed by L. LaSimba M. Gray, Jr., October 12, 2022.
- Burkins, Louetta, daughter of Willie Burkins, Memphis, TN. Interviewed by L. LaSimba M. Gray, Jr., November 3, 2022.
- Hudson, Charles. "Retired Golf Pro at Pine Hill Golf Course." Interviewed by L. LaSimba M. Gray, Jr., October 1, 2022.
- Bryant, Andrew. "Patron of Pine Hill Golf Course," Memphis, Tennessee. Interviewed by L. LaSimba M. Gray, Jr., October 7, 2022.
- Crawford, Robert. "Patron of Pine Hill Golf Course and retired educator." Interviewed by L. LaSimba M. Gray, Jr., November 14, 2022.
- Kennedy, John H. A Course of Their Own: A History of African American Golfers, Lincoln, Nebraska, 2005.
- McDaniels, Pete. Uneven Lies: The Heroic Stories of African Americans in Golf, Greenwich, Connecticut, 2000.

- Crawford, Crenshaw. "Member of the Central State Golfing Association," St. Louis, Missouri. Interviewed by L. LaSimba M. Gray, Jr., June 22, 2022.
- Polk, McCray. "Member of the Memphis Amateur Golf Hall of Fame." Interviewed by L. LaSimba M. Gray, Jr., May 21, 2022.

## PHOTO CREDITS

- Stock images via Adobe Stock
- Pine Hill Photo Album and Hall of Fame Pictures
- Memphis Public Library (Memphis Room)
- Robert Jefferson Coverage of the Golf Tournaments 1970-2023 Memphis Sickle Cell Booster Cub, Courtesy of Mercury Bowie. Robert "Rocky" Jefferson
- Pleas Jones
- Attorney Robert L. Brown Faith Griffin Morris Charles Hudson
- Dr. Harry Davis
- Rev. Louetta Burkins Corneilus Burkins Ruby Fentress
- Charles Sifford -https://www.cleveland.com/open/2014/11/charles_sifford_of_shaker_heig.html
- 1975 AP Wire Photo 1ST BLACK golfer Lee Elder Masters Tournament Augusta Georgia- Wikipwia- By Unknown author (Associated Press) - [1] [2], Public Domain, https://commons.wikimedia.org/w/index.php?curid=69839218

www.ingramcontent.com/pod-product-compliance
Lightning Source LLC
Chambersburg PA
CBHW070102080526
44586CB00013B/1163